CW01090905

Edited by Sally Smith   **May–August 2018**

The Bible Reading Fellowship
15 The Chambers, Vineyard
Abingdon OX14 3FE
brf.org.uk

The Bible Reading Fellowship (BRF) is a Registered Charity (233280)

ISBN 978 0 85746 609 9
All rights reserved

This edition © The Bible Reading Fellowship 2018
Cover image © Sandra Cunningham/Trevillion Images

Acknowledgements

Scripture quotations from The New Revised Standard Version of the Bible, Anglicised edition, copyright © 1989, 1995 by the Division of Christian Education of the National Council of the Churches of Christ in the United States of America. Used by permission. All rights reserved.

Scripture quotations taken from The Holy Bible, New International Version (Anglicised edition) copyright © 1979, 1984, 2011 by Biblica. Used by permission of Hodder & Stoughton Publishers, a Hachette UK company. All rights reserved. 'NIV' is a registered trademark of Biblica. UK trademark number 1448790.

Scripture quotations are taken from THE MESSAGE, copyright © 1993, 1994, 1995, 1996, 2000, 2001, 2002 by Eugene H. Peterson. Used by permission of NavPress. All rights reserved. Represented by Tyndale House Publishers, Inc.

Extract from As a Child by Phil Steer, published by lulu.com, 2012.

Every effort has been made to trace and contact copyright owners for material used in this resource. We apologise for any inadvertent omissions or errors, and would ask those concerned to contact us so that full acknowledgement can be made in the future.

Printed by Gutenberg Press, Tarxien, Malta

Sally Smith writes...

Welcome to *Quiet Spaces*!

I have a quote above my desk from Ann Lamott: 'God loves you exactly as you are, and far too much to leave you as you are.'

It's been there for a few years, but I still keep going back to it. God loves me, warts and all. He knows all those warts, but still loves me. Yet, because he loves me so much, he also sees a better way for me to be me. He isn't going to suddenly change me into that perfect person he knows I can become, but he is longing to work with me to help me on that path.

Fortunately, it isn't dependent on me working hard to become the person God intends me to be. But I do have a part to play in this process. I need to put myself into a situation where I enable God to work within me and I need to allow him to do that work. This means putting myself into God's presence and spending time with him. Like many of you, I know from experience that the better quality the time I offer to God, the better the encounter and the more he is able to work in and with me. As I spend time being his beloved creation, so I become his beloved creation, and that means I become more like the beloved woman he knows I can become.

The closer I get to God, the more I am drawn closer still, and the more I am able to live a life that reflects God's presence with me. It sounds easy, but we know it isn't always straightforward. My prayer is that you are able to use this issue of *Quiet Spaces* to find ways of being with God and encountering him, and that this will lead you closer to becoming the person he longs for you to be. Time spent with God is never wasted, even when it feels like that to us, as he is constantly moulding us more into his likeness, which sounds exciting and awesome.

So allow yourself to be moulded by our creator God and enjoy being in his presence this summer.

Writers in this issue

Janet Fletcher is a priest in the Bro Ystumanner Ministry Area and the Bangor Diocesan Spirituality Officer. She facilitates and offers spiritual direction in the diocese, and enjoys teaching and writing about prayer and spirituality. She has written *Pathway to God* (SPCK, 2006) and has contributed to BRF's *Guidelines* Bible reading notes.

Claire Musters is a freelance writer and editor, mother of two, pastor's wife and school governor. Claire's desire is to help others draw closer to God through her writing, which focuses on marriage, parenting, worship and issues facing women today. To find out more, visit **www.clairemusters.com** and **@CMusters** on Twitter.

Richard Palmer worked previously in HR and training, where he acquired his keen interest in human and spiritual development and vocations. He is Secretary to Derby Diocese Spirituality Group, a spiritual accompanier, writer and runs various courses on the spiritual journey. His passions are family, creative writing and playing the drum kit.

Jean Marie Dwyer OP is a Dominican nun of the Queen of Peace Monastery, Squamish, British Columbia, Canada. The monastery is dedicated to silence, prayer, study and intercession for all people. She is the author of *The Sacred Place of Prayer* (BRF, 2013) and *The Unfolding Journey: The God within: Etty Hillesum and Meister Eckhart* (Novalis, 2014).

Lynne Chitty was a deacon at Gloucester Cathedral and now lives in a caravan in the grounds of Mill House Retreats in Devon. She combines leading creative writing courses with times of solitude and has a variety of rescue animals.

Karen Herrick is a freelance textile artist and creative educator, with a passion for drawing people closer to God through creativity. She works in health and social settings to enhance wellbeing through creativity and runs retreats and quiet days across the Midlands and beyond. Her website is **www.harlequinarts.co.uk**.

Joy McCormick, poet and New Zealand Anglican priest, has special concern for those who struggle to reconcile their experience of Holy Mystery with traditional church doctrine and teaching. Now retired from parish ministry, she continues to offer spiritual direction and supervision and to write. She is author of *Moments of Grace* (BRF, 2013).

Sally Smith enjoys creating spaces that enable encounters with God through leading Quiet Days and creating prayer corners and stations. She has led prayer groups in her local church, works as a spiritual director and writes and produces educational materials.

Having recently retired as a Careers Adviser, **Eirene Palmer** is now enjoying her voluntary work as Diocesan Spiritual Adviser for the Diocese of Derby. She is also a spiritual accompanier and runs courses on aspects of spirituality. Her other passions are writing, family and music, especially singing.

Ruth and Naomi

Janet Fletcher

Introducing Ruth and Naomi

Introduction

The book of Ruth is found between Judges and Samuel. It has only four short chapters and at first it may seem to be a little out of place… or is it? The story of Ruth and Naomi, which took place around 1100 BC, may be one you are already familiar with.

Take time to read the book of Ruth. What are your initial thoughts?

Historically, the story of Ruth (whose name means friendship) comes at the end of the time of the Judges when the tribes of Israel were divided and often strayed away from the covenant relationship with God established through Moses. Following Ruth, the books of Samuel lead to the coming of the kings and to David, Ruth's grandson.

In Matthew's genealogy of Jesus, we read, 'Boaz the father of Obed by Ruth, and Obed the father of Jesse, and Jesse the father of King David' (Matthew 1:5–6; see also Ruth 4:17). It is surprising that Ruth, a Moabite, a foreigner, becomes an important part of this family line.

The book may be named after Ruth, but Naomi also has an important role within the story. The story belongs to them both, and it is a story where the focus is upon the actions and decisions of the two women. The book of Ruth begins with grief and ends with a celebration. It is counter-cultural when compared with Judges and Samuel, which are about the leadership of men, whereas in Ruth, it is the women who lead the way.

Naomi and hospitality

Reflective

As with so many of the stories within the Bible, we are left wondering at all that went on 'behind the scenes'; all the things we'd like to know but the author has left out.

Did Naomi have a place to live in Bethlehem when she returned or was her home offered through the hospitality of a relative? What did Naomi really feel about having Ruth come and live with her? Was Naomi feeling anxious and afraid about returning home and pleased that she had Ruth to give her support? We can only wonder, and perhaps reflect, by putting ourselves into Naomi's place and considering what we would have done and felt.

From the story, though, we know that Naomi offered Ruth hospitality. This was through opening up her home to Ruth, and the way in which she took care of Ruth.

What does the word 'hospitality' mean to you? It is a multifaceted word. It can be a gesture of welcome and acceptance to another person, or the offer of a listening ear. It can be in the sharing of a meal or giving another our warm-hearted attention. It can be through the giving to ourselves 'permission' to take a rest, to seek our own personal space away from the busy-ness of life. It reveals, as Naomi discovers, something of the love of God, leading to a revelation of the indwelling presence of the Holy Spirit.

In a time of quiet prayer:

- Take some time to reflect upon how you, and the church you belong to, can offer hospitality to others. Who has offered you hospitality?
- Take some time to reflect upon how you may give to yourself some hospitality. What would this look like? Is it something you can put into your diary and do?

End this time of prayer by bringing all of your thoughts to God. Ask God to be with you in the hospitality you offer and the hospitality you need to receive – from others and from yourself.

Ruth and belonging

Reflective

When we look at the story of Ruth and all that is not revealed to us, we can wonder about her sense of where she belonged. She obviously felt a love for Naomi, and knew in her heart that her place was to be with Naomi, even though it meant leaving all that was familiar to travel into the unknown. It also meant that she would not know if Bethlehem would be a place where she could belong. To feel a sense of belonging, to belong somewhere, needs acceptance.

John O'Donohue, in his book *Eternal Echoes* (Bantam, 2000), wrote that it is human nature to want to belong. He continues by saying that there are two aspects of belonging. The first is our belonging which he describes as the superficial, 'our external attachment to people, places and things', and secondly, the belonging we seek is one that is 'living and passionate' (p. 3), and draws us to God.

From the story of Ruth, both of these two aspects are present. She wants, and needs, to stay with Naomi, but there is also a far deeper and spiritual call. This call is to follow the God of Naomi. Ruth is willing not only to change and adapt to a new place of living, but also willing to learn about the God of Israel. This deep-rooted call is a call that means she will belong for ever in the ongoing story of the Jewish people, and on into the story of the Christian people.

What does the word 'belonging' mean to you?

A sense of belonging is not static, but moveable and changeable as we grow and learn and settle not simply into a place, but into the 'who we are', into our own personhood and identity.

In a time of quiet prayer:

- Reflect upon times when you have struggled to find a sense of belonging.
- Reflect upon how Ruth's story may help you to understand the two aspects of belonging in your own life.
- At the end of this time of prayer, bring all of your thoughts to God. Ask for God's help to understand more deeply your feelings of belonging, or not belonging.

Moving house

Creative

I have moved house a number of times now, and it doesn't get any easier, which surprises me! Moving house is hard work. Even if the removal firm does all the packing, there is still the unpacking at the end of the journey. I feel that removal firms would get more custom if they included a head and neck massage to ease the stress, and a manicure to heal broken nails and roughened hands after pulling sticky tape off boxes! Maybe you have experienced a house move that makes you shudder at the thought of it.

Naomi and Ruth no doubt moved house with very little, perhaps with only the things they could carry. Nonetheless, it was still probably hard work for them.

There is an excitement to moving house. A new place to live, new people to get to know and new experiences hopefully to enjoy.

When you have the space and time, bring with you into a time of prayer big or small sheets of paper, pencils and crayons.

Firstly, become quiet with God, in the way you find best.

Then be creative in words, doodles and pictures. Draw a house, perhaps the rooms of your house. Then write or draw what you feel is really precious to you from each of those rooms. With a different colour, write or draw the things that if needed you could do without.

In the quietness of prayer, give thanks to God for all the precious objects and the memories those rooms hold for you.

In the quietness of prayer, ask God to help you let go of the things that you do not need.

Write down anything that you sense is important to reflect more upon at another time.

Finish this time of prayer, knowing that God is with you.

Journey with God

Prayer

In a time of quietness, pray through the words below. Is there anything that strikes you as important or relating to your own journey with God? Make a note of how you feel, what feels comfortable or disturbs, what comes to mind, and anything that you sense is calling you to bring it back into prayer at another time.

When I hesitate on my journey with you, my God,
may the voice of Ruth call me back and fill my ears,
'Where you go, I will go.'
When I stray on my journey with you, my God,
may the voice of Ruth call me back and fill my heart,
'Your God, my God.'
When I wander on my journey with you, my God,
may the voice of Ruth call me back and fill my life,
'Where you lodge, I will lodge.'
In all of my hesitating, straying and wandering,
I know you are my God and I am yours.

You have called deep into my life to come and follow,
and in my growing and deepening faith I hear your call.
I will journey with you, my God,
for wherever I am
I know that you are present with me.
I will journey with you, my God,
for when I seek forgiveness
I know that you bring your love to me.
I will journey with you, my God,
for whenever I become distracted
I know that you are with me still for you abide within me.
Amen

Who is family?

Reflective

What makes up a family today? Family is very different today from how it was in previous generations, and particularly from the understanding of family at the time of Ruth and Naomi. In the biblical time of the Old Testament, family was regarded as being more than a single group of parents, in-laws and children. Families who shared a common ancestor came together as a clan, and from there to being a part of a tribe, tracing their ancestry back to one of the twelve sons of Jacob.

For Naomi, who had no more sons to be a husband for Ruth, the issue of carrying on the family name was very important, for it was the family name that gave them both present and future hope. For Naomi, this is 'solved' in Ruth's marriage to Boaz, a kinsman. As he wasn't the next in line, the next of kin, he needed to plead his case, as we read in chapter 4, before he could take Ruth as his wife. To be family also meant being under the headship and leadership of the father, uncle, brother or son.

Since those days, there has been a massive social sift, even in the last hundred years or so. Then, families rarely left their family unit or clan. They stayed together and looked after each other. Later in our history, families may not have lived under the same roof, but often in the same street or neighbourhood. Today, families often live far apart, and sometimes in different parts of the world. Families can include stepchildren, may be made of a group of friends, or may be through being a single parent.

What effect do you think these various ways of being family would have on the family members?

What is the make-up of your family? Is it a close family regardless of distance between members, or does it include members you have no contact with?

The church, and our belonging to and in God, is also a family, a family of believers. How important is it to you to be a part of the family of your church? What do you think the church could do to help in family life? And, the other way around, what can families teach the church?

On the edge

Reflective

As we have seen, Ruth is an outsider, a foreigner. She was determined though to go with Naomi, and take the risk of being excluded and distrusted. Ruth could easily have been shunned by the community and people wary and suspicious of her strange and foreign ways.

There would have been cultural, social and religious differences that Ruth would need to overcome, and yet she is adamant and willing to learn everything about the place she now lives in. Ruth is the refugee, even though she is given a home with Naomi. Naomi becomes the welcoming and nurturing 'stranger' even though they are already family. They help each other, and no doubt Naomi learns as much from Ruth as Ruth learns from Naomi.

Today, refugees and asylum seekers still come to us through the media, and perhaps more closely within the communities we live in.

Does your church offer support to, or work with, other agencies to help refugees and asylum seekers?

Refugees are only one group of people who live on the edge, as 'labelled' perhaps by society. Maybe in your area there are people who are homeless, people in need of food from the food bank, people unable to work because of disability, people named as troublemakers to be avoided.

What can you do to help, and what can or does your church do to help?

How could you be as Naomi, a welcoming and nurturing person, to those who live 'on the edge'?

Naomi – her story

Story

I am a woman with a story to tell. I have experienced love and joy, and the sorrow that grief brings. I have been a respected woman in my village and I have been a 'no one'. Returning to Bethlehem was difficult. I had left so many years ago and death brought me home; a life empty of husband and sons. Why did this happen?

Out of the sorrow came joy. I was not totally empty and alone, for Ruth, my daughter-in-law, decided to come with me. She left her family and all that was familiar, including the gods she worshipped. I tried to persuade her not to come with me, but she was, and is, a very determined woman.

Now I am home amongst my kinsfolk. I was concerned about Ruth and whether the people here would accept her. She went to glean and gather the leftovers from a family field, but I warned her to take care. I needn't have worried, for my kinsman Boaz watched over her. When I saw his interest grow, I encouraged Ruth to return it.

She can't live alone; she's too young. She needs a husband to watch over her, keep her safe from other men when I am no longer living. It brings me joy in my heart again as I look at Ruth with Boaz. The family name of my husband and sons will continue now as my hope for a grandson will come to me from Ruth.

I am a woman with a story to tell. I could not stand aside as men came to barter for her. I did whatever I could to ensure she is safe and cared for. After all she has done for me, I thank God for her, and know that she is and will be blessed in her life.

- Look back over your life – how have the joys and the sorrows experienced changed, challenged or transformed you? Where was God in this?
- Naomi lived in a very different cultural and social age to ours. Whatever your age is, reflect upon the cultural and social changes that have taken place – are these ones you welcome and embrace, or not?

Ruth – her story

Story

I am a woman with a story to tell. By so many I am seen as a foreigner, an outsider. People are wary of me, a widow, although Naomi has helped me gain a little acceptance. She can be very protective! Why did I decide to follow Naomi, to give up, surrender my previous life? I'm not sure, except it felt it was the right thing to do.

If I had returned to my family, my father would have married me quickly and I would have had no say in it at all. Staying with Naomi means I gain some independence and can make my own decisions and not have them made for me. Naomi was surprised I was determined to go with her. I wanted to, and I wanted to learn about her God. I suppose I was hungry for something I felt was missing in my life, and now I had the chance to feed that hunger. I had no idea what my future would hold. If I'd been told, I don't think I would have believed it.

When I went to glean in the fields, I met Naomi's kinsman, Boaz, who made sure I would be safe. Naomi was thrilled I'd met him and she encouraged me, pushed me even, to go and lie at his feet. Why did I? I could have said no, but he was a kind man, and if I was to survive here I needed to be married; and I'd rather it was him than any other. I knew too, how important this was for Naomi.

I am a woman with a story to tell. As far as I can, I will make my own decisions. Have I, though, or have I simply followed the traditions and customs of this time? To ensure my future, did I opt for the easiest way open to me? I don't think so, because I feel in my heart that my decision to follow Naomi was important, and so too my marriage to Boaz. I trust in Naomi's God, who is mine as well now, to reveal at the right time what these feelings in my heart mean.

- How do you make decisions in life? What part does faith play in your decision making?
- Ruth placed her trust in Naomi and in God. How easy or difficult is it to trust another person, and to trust in God?

This is my story

Prayer

Ruth and Naomi have 'told' their stories. In this time of quiet prayer, ponder over how you would tell your own story. You may wish to write or draw images to reflect different stages of your life, or use the prayer below to help you pick out particular moments that you remember.

Is this a story you would want to share with anyone else? Or is this a story you would prefer to keep for yourself? Ruth and Naomi made their own decisions. So, too, it is your decision whether or not you share your prayer and story.

At the end of the prayer, offer it all to God and know that the love of God is with you.

O God,
I know deep within you have planted the story of faith,
deep into my life.
The story of my life is entwined with yours,
and I ask your presence to be with me now
as I bring into the light the precious moments,
the difficult times and joy-filled times.
For this is my life:
There are times in my story when I did not make good decisions.
There are times in my life when I know I made the right decision.
There are times in my life when I have been surprised
at the direction my decisions have led me.
There are times when I have cried and laughed,
been sad and happy, frustrated and content, angry and at peace.
For all of these times, and so many more, I thank you, O God.
For this is me and this my story, and I know you are deep within
each and every memory that has shaped the story of my life.
Thank you, O God. Amen

Belonging in God

Reflective

For Ruth, to belong meant belonging to the God of Naomi. Deep within the story of our faith, and the interconnected story of our life, is the call, the need to belong. We belong in a multitude of ways to different groups, friend networks, places of work, and within a family. With faith and through our baptism is our belonging that is rooted in God, and from there the church communities which we are a part of.

Ruth had made the decision to go with Naomi, to not only belong with Naomi but also to belong to the God of Israel. We are not told how Ruth grew in her faith and understanding of God, nor how, or if, she came to realise a sense of belonging in God.

What do you understand by the phrase 'belonging in God' within your own journey of faith?

What does this phrase mean to you in relation to your own prayer and spirituality?

What do you understand by this phrase in relation to the wider church?

Belonging and a sense of belonging touches into our inner being, and into our inner well-being. To believe that we belong in God can bring comfort, hope, peace and love that will provide an inner strength when our 'belonging' in the world causes us to struggle, to be anxious and uncertain.

Belonging in God brings us acceptance and love, and leads the way towards living a life of integrity, welcome, justice and peace. Deepening our inner life through this belonging in God will nourish and refresh us, open our hearts to God's ongoing call to us, and enable us to discern the path in life we are to follow.

How may you deepen your belonging in God?

Who may be able to help you to do this?

Drawing the story together

Bible study

Read again the book of Ruth.

What thoughts come to you now, and are they different or the same as when you first read the book of Ruth?

Towards the end of the book of Ruth, we read of the people calling to the Lord that, when Ruth and Boaz come together in marriage, she will build up the house of Israel (4:11). They would no doubt be very surprised at the way that Ruth did build up the people of Israel! In her marriage, her story began to take on a new direction in the birth of Obed. It also meant that she gave to Naomi status and the continuation of the family name.

A few generations later, her grandson David would be named king and find himself in trouble with Saul. This, though, is another story (read 1 Samuel 16 onwards if you are interested). The story which runs from Ruth to David and onwards to us is the coming of Jesus, and the genealogy takes Jesus' family line back to Ruth.

We are the inheritors of Ruth's love and willingness to travel with her mother-in-law to a different place. Ruth, along with Naomi, was open to God's presence, even unknowingly perhaps, but willing, as Mary was so many centuries later, to answer with a 'yes' the tug on her heart, the call of God.

What has challenged you as you've journeyed with Ruth and Naomi?

What have you learnt from the story of Ruth and Naomi that may help you in your own life?

How does, or has, God tugged at your heart? Where did that lead you to?

Being mindful

Claire Musters

Mindful of God's presence

Introduction

I recently co-presented a seminar entitled 'Mindful of God's presence'. It looked at the recent rise of interest in mindfulness, and how Christians in particular are engaging with it. Mindfulness can be described as paying attention to the present moment in a non-judgemental way.

It was scientific research into the benefits of mindfulness skills for our wellbeing that brought the subject to the fore in recent years, and it is now recommended by the Department of Health (particularly for treating depression). Many Christians are also recognising the benefits of using mindfulness techniques in their own daily spiritual walk.

Learning to be more mindful involves slowing ourselves down for long enough to be more aware of what is going on around us. This simple exercise will help you to do this:

1 **Stop**
   Simply stop whatever you are doing. You may find it helpful to sit in a comfortable position.

2 **Observe**
   Give attention to the here and now: observe what is around you; note any movements; observe any sounds you hear. Begin to observe what is happening to your 'self' too:

- Note the experience of physical sensations in your body.
- Observe your thoughts, feelings, emotions – simply acknowledging them rather than trying to change them.
- Give yourself permission to accept that there is nothing you need to do in this moment.

3 Focus on your breathing

Spend some time simply observing your breathing. Focus on your inwards breath filling your whole body, from top to toe, and then on your outwards breath, feeling the breath leave your body (like the action of bellows). If any thoughts, feelings or distractions come in, try not to judge them – just gently bring your attention back to your breathing by noting any emotions that come alongside the thoughts and then letting them all go.

4 Return

This final step broadens your attention back out to whatever is going on around you, while trying to keep connected to a sense of calmness.

Being able to stop and be attentive to the present moment in this way can have huge benefits for those who are suffering from stress, depression, etc. Slowing down is of great benefit to all of us, and many Christians recognise that there are elements within mindfulness that reflect ancient Christian traditions and biblical principles. For example, as we've seen above, focusing on breathing is a big part of mindfulness but also of Christian meditation.

Co-writing three CWR *Insight Guides* with a counsellor, in which we looked at mindfulness, pricked my interest in the subject. However, I had already been drawn to look at some of the older writers on contemplative prayer in my own devotional times. Coming from a vibrant, lively evangelical background, I have begun to recognise the need for regular quiet, rest and refreshment in my life. I can see that there is much I can learn from the writings and practices of older, more monastic approaches.

I am not focusing purely on Christian mindfulness here, but am drawing on the various sources that have helped me personally to be more mindful of God.

Ever mindful of us

Reflective/creative

The psalmist says, 'What is mankind that you are mindful of them?' (Psalm 8:4). The word 'mindful' comes from the Greek word, *mimneske*, which means 'to be mindful of'. The Hebrew word *zakar*, which is translated as 'be mindful' in English Bibles has a range of meanings that include 'remember', 'keep in mind', 'call to mind', 'be concerned about' and 'meditate'. This describes a kind of loving attentiveness.

God's basic nature is to be mindful towards us – caring and loving, hospitable, refraining from judging until the appropriate moment. Think of the father's response when the prodigal returns in Luke 15:20–24. While God will judge all the earth, as described in Revelation 20:11–15, his response when we turn towards him is always loving.

In Isaiah 49:15–16 God describes his mindful attitude towards us beautifully:

> *Can a mother forget the baby at her breast*
> *and have no compassion on the child she has borne?*
> *Though she may forget,*
> *I will not forget you!*
> *See, I have engraved you on the palms of my hands;*
> *your walls are ever before me.*

Take some time to sit quietly and reflect on the fact that you are engraved on the palms of God's hands. It may help you to hold your own palms in front of you, and imagine God's, bigger and full of the names that he has written on them – including your own.

You may also like to either download and print out a picture of hand palms and then write your name across them, or draw your own hands and then add your name.

You can then use this visual reminder throughout the coming days to focus on the wonderful truth that you are engraved on the palm of God's hands; that he is ever mindful of you, and ever loving towards you.

The Jesus Prayer

Prayer

The Jesus Prayer is the earliest recorded prayer that focused on meditating *on* Jesus. It goes like this:

Lord Jesus Christ, Son of God, have mercy on me.

The words are based on those of the tax collector found in Luke 18:13. It was used in early traditions as an anchor prayer, a means of anchoring a person's attention towards God. The phrase was repeated, in order to set aside worry and worldly concerns, as a kind of preparation – to turn the heart towards prayer.

Take some time to engage with the Jesus Prayer yourself today:

Firstly, find a comfortable place to sit. You may find it helpful to close your eyes. Relax, and then simply and slowly repeat the line as many times as you would like to:

Lord Jesus Christ, Son of God, have mercy on me.

When you are ready to finish, take some time to reflect on how you responded to the phrase as you were praying it. Was there a particular word that stood out when you repeated the prayer? Or a new insight into how you view Jesus perhaps? Did you have a sense of Jesus' mercy pouring onto you afresh?

Take your response to God in thankful prayer.

Being and doing

Story

'Wow! He's asked to come here – for us to host a gathering of him and his closest friends. What an honour. But what a lot to do and so little time to do it in. We must get going quickly!'

'I need to write a list. Think of all the food I need to buy. There's so few hours – and look at the mess! We really must *get on with clearing up too, and making the house look presentable. What is Mary doing? She needs to help or I'll never be ready!*

'I wonder if I'll get a chance to listen to him? I've so longed to sit near him and hear what he has to say. He is intriguing – his very words seem to breathe life to those around him...'

'Mary! What are you doing? Stop daydreaming and help me! I don't know how we are going to get everything done!'

I wonder how you respond when Jesus asks to come and spend some time with you. Above, I simply imagined what could have been going through Martha's and Mary's thoughts in the short time before Jesus arrived at their home – and some of what Martha could have said in the panic of preparation.

Read through Luke 10:38–42, while reflecting on the fact that Jesus responded to the frantic 'doing' of Martha by saying that

Mary had chosen the better part by 'being' with him.

There can often be such a tussle between doing and being and I think this is exaggerated because our society is so geared up to 'doing'. But it is important that we intentionally take time out, balancing the rushing around with a sense of quiet calm, because being mindful of Jesus necessitates a slowing down, to simply 'be' with him.

Think about the ways in which you can 'be' with Jesus today – to invite him into your 'spiritual' home, your heart, afresh. What may you need to lay aside in order to choose the better way?

Bible verse colouring

Creative

There are a plethora of colouring books on the market these days, and it is easy to see why as it is so enjoyable. Not only that, but using our fine motor skills for an activity such as colouring can really help us focus our minds to be attentive. Taking a verse, writing it out and then doodling and colouring around and in it can really help us to concentrate on what is being said in the verse.

To start your own Bible verse colouring, choose a verse – perhaps one that reveals something of God's character (such as Psalm 145:8). Take time to write it out carefully – you may like to use block capitals or 'bubble' writing so that you can draw and colour inside the letters as well as around them. (If you would prefer, you could create the verse 'template' on your computer, or do an online search for verses suitable for colouring in, which you can then simply print out – although I would say engaging with writing the verse out is a helpful part of the experience.) Then spend time with the verse, doodling your response to it and colouring in as you do so.

Once you have finished your Bible verse colouring, put it up somewhere so that you can keep looking at it over the next few days.

Awareness through the ordinary/ Practising the presence of God

Spotlight

Throughout history, there have been figures who have suggested that becoming mindful of Christ's presence throughout our ordinary, day-to-day lives helps us to become more like him. Brother Lawrence (c. 1611–91), for example, a lay brother in the Carmelite order, outlined a series of exercises for practising his awareness of God's presence while undertaking kitchen duties in the monastry. He called it 'practising the presence of God' and suggested that people should be able to pray wherever they are at any time of day or night.

More recently, Frank Laubach (1884–1970), educator and missionary, advocated a 'game with minutes', recommending that Christians experiment with keeping God in mind for at least a second in every minute.

Why not find a way to engage with the ideas for keeping God in mind that these historical figures introduce us to? Perhaps you could set an alarm to go off every half an hour or hour, and take five minutes to engage more intentionally with God. Or you could take some time to write a list of the daily chores you undertake and then decide to find new ways to converse with God as you do them.

Gospel contemplation

Imaginative

One of the ways that we can interact with the Bible afresh, while seeking to be mindful of Jesus as we do so, is by engaging in imaginative contemplation of a passage in which Jesus is present. We can try and use all our senses as we do so. Here is a general introduction of how to do this:

- Select a passage where Jesus is interacting with others.
- Read it a few times until it becomes familiar.
- Close your eyes and recreate the scene in your mind. What does the scene look like? What does it smell like? Be mindful of how people are interacting with one another, how Jesus looks and how people are reacting to him. What are people saying? What emotions are being expressed? Is Jesus reaching out to someone?
- Move on to imagine yourself entering the scene. How do you interact with others? With Jesus?
- Reflect on how the scene makes you feel and what you feel you need/want from Jesus. Speak to him from the heart in prayer before finishing.

Use the passage below, or set it aside and choose another biblical scene yourself.

If you are particularly artistic, you may like to try drawing the scene once you have visualised it. This will give you something to come back to for further contemplation another time (and colouring it in, or painting it, will give you more opportunity to be mindful of your response to it).

Sit comfortably and read through Matthew 14:13–21 a few times.

Close your eyes and try to recreate the scene. What does it look like, with the crowds of people trying to get to Jesus? Are they jostling with one another, or sitting patiently? How are the disciples feeling? Are they weary and wanting to rest? How do they respond to Jesus? How do they respond to the people, when Jesus asks the disciples to feed them? Are they gracious or not? How do the people respond to being fed? Do any try and thank Jesus personally? How do the disciples feel when they see the miracle that Jesus has performed?

Now imagine you are in the crowd, perhaps desperately craning to see Jesus as his boat arrives on the shore. Do you push forward, eager to see him? Do you get angry with those in front of you, or do you relax and enjoy the moment, of being with others in the crowd and anticipating hearing from Jesus? What about when the disciples begin to bring around bread and fish? Which disciple passes some to you? What interaction do you have with them? How does the bread and fish smell – and taste? Once you have eaten well, do you have a chance to speak to Jesus, or does he speak to the crowd at all?

Take some time to reflect on how contemplating on that passage made you feel. Is there something in particular you feel you want to ask Jesus now? Take your thoughts to him in prayer.

As if for the first time…

Going out

Learning to see things around us as if for the first time helps us to focus on God's creation and all its glory. While I have recently learned that having what is called 'a beginner's mind' is a key attitude of mindfulness, God was teaching me the benefits of this over a decade ago. My daughter is almost secondary school-aged, but when God spoke to me about this, she was a toddler.

We set out one day, soon after she had learned to walk, and I was getting frustrated because it was taking for ever just to get to the end of our road (which is very short!). This was because my daughter stopped to look at everything in amazement – a crack in a pavement, a ladybird on a lamppost, the tufts of grass trying to grow through the concrete.

I began to get more and more worked up as I tried to chivvy her along when God gently asked me to stop. He instructed me to get down to her eye level and experience the world afresh, like she was. It was an incredibly eye-opening moment for me, and one that I try and remind myself of often. Experiencing the richness of the present moment, which we invariably take for granted, helps us to be truly alive. It also creates the possibility of discovering new things within environments very well known to us.

So why not take a walk of mindfulness today, whether simply along your street or in a park or other open space?

Take your time, and, as you start, ask God to open your eyes to discover things afresh, as if for the first time. Then be attentive to the little details, such as an insect hovering over a flower, or a bird flying overhead.

As you draw your walk to an end, thank God for the natural world, and for the fresh perspective he has given you today.

Be still and know

Meditative

Give your entire attention to what God is doing right now, and don't get worked up about what may or may not happen tomorrow. God will help you deal with whatever hard things come up when the time comes.

MATTHEW 6:34 (MSG)

As we can see in the verse above, Jesus instructed his disciples to live in the present, rather than worrying about what might happen in the future. It is so easy, isn't it, to start (and end!) a week by getting caught up with all the things that we have to do. It can cause our stress levels to rise, and our body can respond by not sleeping well, our heart rate rising, etc. But if we take time to slow down, bringing our anxieties to Jesus (even visualising leaving them at the foot of the cross for him to deal with), and focus on the moment, we can learn to stop allowing so much to crowd our minds.

Even before Jesus walked the earth, God said: 'Be still, and know that I am God' (Psalm 46:10). It is important that we take the time

27

to do so. Here is a basic outline of one way in which you can try to engage with this:

Find a quiet spot in the house, sit down and intentionally relax. Allow all the tension that has begun to build up as you think of the tasks for the day to flow out, and centre your attention on God.

It can be helpful to concentrate on your breathing. Slowing it down a little aids relaxation. As you breathe in, you may like to say 'Be', and as you breathe out, say 'still'. You could move on to using the phrase 'Come rest' or any other phrase that comes to mind.

Having relaxed in this way, we are often much more open to sensing the presence and peace of God. Sit in this state for as long as you are able and then, before moving on, invite God's guidance, so that you understand what it is that he would have you do in the day ahead.

If you prefer taking time out to be with God in the evening, you can utilise a similar routine of being still and relaxing. The Ignatian spiritual exercise, the Daily Examen, is one that many Christians use to look back over a day to discern where God was in the midst of it.

To do this, take time to intentionally review the events of the day, thanking God for the people you interacted with and any small details that come to mind. Pay particular attention to your thoughts and emotions and how they changed. Were there moments when God felt close by? Any times when he seemed absent? Were there times when you recognise that you resisted him? What can you learn from this?

Pick one moment to think about more closely, either because it was a significant encounter or it caused positive or negative emotions. Pray about it in whichever way seems right (i.e. intercession, praise, repentance, etc.) before letting it go and thanking God generally for the gift of the day you have just had.

Reflective prayer

Prayer

One of the fresh ways we can engage with prayer is through taking a verse of scripture and spending time with it. Once you have chosen a verse, observe the thoughts and feelings that arise as you read it, and the bodily sensations (such as relaxation) you experience (much as you did with the starting exercise). You can then incorporate your observations into your prayers.

Here are a few verses you might like to utilise:

Great is the Lord and most worthy of praise.
PSALM 145:3

He is my loving God and my fortress, my stronghold and my deliverer.
PSALM 144:2

Below is the prayer that resulted from my experience with the second verse. Feel free to use it as a starting point or create your own.

God you are loving and caring,
I thank you that I can call you my God and Father.
You are my fortress – that place I can run to and hide when life is getting too much.
I can pour out my pain, my fears and my worries – and find security and comfort in return.
I know that you will protect me and keep me, and ultimately deliver me from the evil that seems to be all around.
I can stand strong in you, knowing that you are solid and unshakeable.

I trust you.
Thank you Lord, for who you are.
Amen

Lectio divina

Meditative

Lectio divina is a particular way of reading the Bible slowly. It is most closely associated with Benedict of Nursa (c. 480–545) although it was further developed in the twelfth century.

There are various approaches, but most divide it into four steps (some refer to these as the four 'r's of reading, reflection, response and rest):

- *lectio*: reading the passage (a few times – including out loud to hear what the passage sounds like).
- *meditatio*: reflection and meditation on the passage (chewing it over).
- *oratio*: response or prayers for guidance on the passage from the Holy Spirit, leaving our thinking aside for the moment to allow our hearts to respond to God.
- *contemplatio*: rest – our usual assumptions about what a passage means are intentionally suspended (the beginner's mind approach again). We let go of our own ideas, plans and thoughts and simply rest in the passage. This contemplation can also move on to pay attention to which phrase comes most into mind. This phrase is then accepted as a gift, rather than something that we need to engage with and analyse further.

Rather than being too prescriptive, I would invite you now to choose a passage of scripture for yourself and then try reading it using the four steps of *lectio divina*.

Being mindful box

Creative

End this section by thinking about all the things that you have learned while engaging with being intentionally more mindful of God. There may have been particular insights you gained while meditating on a passage, or perhaps as you walked outside observing the natural world. Thank God for the precious new gifts he has given you as you have been doing this.

Take some time to write down these insights on pieces of paper; feel free to ultilise the colouring/doodling approach as you do so.

Then either make or decorate a simple box, which will become your 'being mindful' box. You could, for example, wrap a shoebox in colourful paper, or buy a cheap box and add extra decorations to it.

Once finished, place the bits of paper into the box. You can continue to add to the box over time and also dip back into it, taking out a piece of paper to remind yourself of what you've learned.

The greatness of God – how big is God?

Richard Palmer

Introduction

Creative

How big is God? It sounds like a question a young child would ask. But actually, a good few of us would have to give off-the-cuff dismissive answers because it is one of those out-of-the-mouths-of-babes-and-sucklings questions. In other words, it is a very good question. Read Isaiah 40:28, noting the phrase 'his understanding is unsearchable'. In other words, God is too big to understand.

Think about your own image of God. Take a piece of blank A4 paper and draw up to four squares or picture frames on it. You can get artistic with the frames if you like. Now draw, as best as you can, your images of God over your lifetime. Start in your early years at say five years old and draw a picture of God in the first square. Finish with your image as of today. In between these two images, depending upon your age, you may have one or two different images you would like to draw. When complete, use the images to reflect upon your changing views of the size and nature of God over your lifetime.

Our personal confusion with images of God starts when we are young. We learn about Christ the Son, and his Father. We hear of Christ sitting at the right hand of God. We also read that God made us in his image. These are all physical bodily images. Hence the cartoon image of a God on a throne with a beard is not surprising. These, together with our early childhood thoughts of God as a

Father Christmas figure, who grants all our wishes, sets us up for failure in later life as we try to consider the question of the size of God.

Notice that we are thinking about *size*. We do this because we want to give God a frame. We need a container to keep him in and a picture we can hold in our minds and work with. But as John 4:24 tells us, 'God is spirit'. In 1 John 4:8 we learn that God is love. If we can grasp these two images of God as spirit and love, we are starting to move towards a more realistic possible vision of God.

God is also omnipotent and omnipresent. If you or I were present everywhere, we would be very thinly spread. But the key is that God's presence is not diluted. We don't just get half a per cent of him because he's off somewhere else attending to another important matter. We get all of God. Once again, 'his understanding is unsearchable'.

Putting God in a box

Creative

As humans, we like boxes and the order they bring. They help us manage our lives. We live in our homes and sit in our gardens. We travel in our cars and we store things in our cupboards. These boxes help us to categorise things, giving us a manageable edge to our existence and making it self-contained. If we looked out of our back window and the garden was just a never-ending expanse of land, we'd have no ownership or sense of place. In order to know it is ours, we fence it off and own it.

When it comes to forming an image of an omnipresent and omnipotent God, human imagination cannot cope with the enormity of this idea. We have to put some parameters around it. Thus begins the process of boxing God in, so that we can manage and handle him.

Take a blank sheet of A4 paper (or card) and some masking tape. The paper represents your life. Make a shape with the masking tape on the paper. Inside write the areas of life where you let God in. Outside the boundaries of the shape, write the areas where you don't let God in. Another way of thinking about this is to consider how much you really trust God. Do you give everything to him? Or do you think that God won't be able to sort that bit out or do it the way you want, so you'd better do it instead? What is the size of God's box, his garden in your life? You can move the masking tape to make the area larger or smaller. If you have no tape, draw pencil lines that can be erased and changed.

Are there areas of life you'd like to open up to God? Name them. (If you are stuck for ideas, consider these broad categories of our daily lives – leisure, relationships, finance, health, career, home, family.) Or do others box God in for you? Who are they?

The nature of God

Visual/imaginative

Our images of God are also ruled by our images of God's nature. It is so simple to give a problem to God in prayer and give him the answer too. We know precisely what we want and how it should happen.

Read Isaiah 55:8–9.

If you have ever owned a pet, part of the joy is watching their different perceptions of life and how they understand the world. For instance, pets do not understand the dangers of crossing the road or how escape from their safe pet enclosure can bring extreme danger. Their reasoning capabilities are much lower than ours, and so it is with God and us; we cannot understand his broader view of the world and our place within it.

We only have a small view of the entirety; we see the community in which we breathe and move. Consider the huge panorama that our Lord God has. Imagine the shots sometimes seen on TV, of a camera zooming out from a house to a street, then to a town, a country, then out to the world and off into space.

Do this in your imagination or on Google maps satellite view. Start in your house and zoom out. In a few clicks, you are out in outer space. Let God journey with you and listen to him as he views what you see.

Prayer sizes – small, medium, large, extra large

Prayer

'The Lord works in mysterious ways, his wonders to perform.' It is a commonly uttered phrase and it underlines the mystery and the power of our creator God. We are limited in our understanding of God by the size of our own human intellect.

The Artist's Way by Julia Cameron (Pan, 1995) sets out to help the reader discover their creative self and banish their self-doubt and criticism. In the course of the book, she has this to say on God as the source of power and creativity:

> Most of us never consider how powerful the creator really is. Instead, we draw very limited amounts of the power available to us. We decide how powerful God is for us. We unconsciously set a limit on how much God can give us or help us. And if we receive a gift beyond our imagining, we often send it back.

It is an interesting point to reflect upon. Do you limit your prayers to God on the basis that God is only capable of so much or that it is a bit impolite to ask for more?

Take time to consider the prayers of your church community. Are there prayers in your church that are too small? For instance, a church may spend an inordinate amount of time and prayer on choosing the exact shade of colour for the church redecoration. A bigger prayer may be to offer to God the fact that they are redecorating in hope of reaching out to the local community. Are they governing the answers to prayer by making their prayers too small?

Write a large prayer for your church community. Read it again and ask God how you can make the prayer bigger. Rewrite it in its bigger form. Try again – can you make it bigger still? Are you still able to pray to the big God for your big prayer? Are you ready for big answers?

Apples and oranges

Meditative

Often when I pray, I tell God exactly what I want to happen and what the answer is, just in case he hasn't understood the answer that I want. In Julia Cameron's book *The Artist's Way* (Pan, 1995), she talks of the issues of having trust in and loving our internal guide (God). In other words, can I trust God or do I need to do this myself?

She says this:

This concept is a very hard one for most of us to really credit. We tend to believe we must go out and shake a few trees to make things happen. I would not deny that shaking a few trees is good for us. In fact, I believe it is necessary. I call it doing the footwork. I want to say, however, that while the footwork is necessary, I have seldom seen it pay off in a linear fashion. It seems to work more like we shake the apple tree and the universe delivers oranges.

God operates in a mysterious fashion as opposed to our logical human way of answering a problem. Spend some time reflecting on how you have experienced shaking apple trees and getting oranges.

Think of times when your prayers have been answered in an unexpected or unusual way. If you keep a prayer or spiritual journal, you may find evidence in there. If you don't, make a habit of noting your prayer requests in a diary or journal to see what is answered and how. A further idea is to post an important prayer into an envelope and stick it in a drawer. Open it six months to a year later and see if and how it has been answered and see if it is what you expected.

The universe

Reflective

Up until the early 1600s, most people were happy to believe that the earth sat at the centre of the universe and the Sun and the universe revolved around us. Galileo thought otherwise and published his findings, proclaiming that the earth orbited the Sun. This didn't work out well for him. He was tried in 1615, accused of heresy and held under house arrest for the rest of his life.

The problem was that the established church previously had God and the universe neatly packaged in a nice little box. The scriptures could be interpreted to say the earth was central and they didn't want any scientist coming along and upsetting the celestial apple cart, which is precisely what Galileo did. It was a revolutionary idea, but it was, of course, correct. It caused much debate about the nature of God.

Have there been times in your life when your views of God have been shaken up – a major life event, a change of church, a time of illness or another substantial occurrence? Such times are never comfortable, but often, afterwards, there is growth. Reflect upon how your views of God changed at these times, for better or for worse and how you felt about this. You can write about this in your journal or draw an image to represent this event.

More about the universe

Creative

Here are some current discoveries and beliefs about our universe. Our earth sits in a galaxy called the Milky Way and current estimates are that there may be about 100–400 billion stars in our galaxy. The Sun is our star, so that is a lot of suns in the Milky Way. Therefore, our galaxy is a humungously vast place.

If we go beyond our galaxy, how many other galaxies are there? The previous estimate was approximately 200 billion galaxies. However, in October 2016, the Hubble telescope revealed that the universe contains 10 times more galaxies than previously thought, that is, 2,000 billion galaxies. The population of the earth has now reached seven billion. That's 285 galaxies for each person on earth. Remember also that each galaxy contains 100–400 billion stars. It is at this point that the size of the universe really does become unfathomable.

Take a level teaspoon of rice and scatter it on a dark surface. Colour one grain with a felt-tip pen in a bright contrasting colour. This coloured grain is our galaxy, the Milky Way.

A teaspoonful of basmati rice is approximately 300 grains. Call it 285! The grains of rice scattered on your surface are your own personal number of galaxies. Everyone on earth has a similar teaspoonful of galaxies. If God has created such a vast panorama of a universe, how big can God possibly be? Read Psalm 147:4 and meditate upon the God who names the stars.

Wide vistas and small details

Reflective

Read Matthew 10:29–31 and Psalm 147:4. Reflect upon the mightiness of our God who creates and names the stars and yet also numbers the hairs upon our heads.

Take a flower or find an image of a flower. I have a rock rose in bloom at present. It has translucent white petals like crêpe paper and five dark maroon splodges of colour towards its yellow centre. It is a thing of immense beauty, and blooms but a day. Spend time looking at the immense detail that exists in your flower.

Contrast God's concern for the detail with the vastness of the known universe. It is estimated that there are 2,000 billion galaxies. We believe we are getting an understanding of space and yet, in the history of man, six manned landings on the Moon between 1969 and 1972 is the measure of our trips to other parts of the universe. The myth of mankind conquering space is very far away. We must remember *Star Trek* is science fiction.

There is huge mystery in the creation of the universe, both in its size and nature. God's cosmic creation mirrors the power and might of God. Find a quiet, comfortable space to sit and reflect on a God of such power, who numbers the hairs upon your head. Sense how important you are to God.

The wind blows

Reflective

God is so big that we need to put a frame around him to try to understand his nature and power. With that need to understand also comes the need to control. We'd like to control God a bit, because who knows what God may get up to otherwise? We know it can only be good, but will it be what we want it to be?

Likewise, throughout history, religious institutions have insisted upon rules and regulations, claiming that only they know the God-given truth, and putting God into a neatly packaged set of rules, seeking to control both God and their followers. Such control can be extremely dangerous and gives those involved the power to control people and their beliefs. It was only in the 16th century through the actions of Tyndale, Martin Luther and King Henry VIII that the wider population could read the Bible for the first time in their own language, rather than in Latin.

Our individual relationship and sense of understanding of God can be restricted by the rulings and interpretations of others. But we are given the gift of the Holy Spirit to guide us. God does not leave the governing of the heavenly kingdom on earth solely in the hands of religion. The spirit with which we are imbued leads us on and guides us.

Read John 3:5–8. Contemplate upon the meaning of flesh versus spirit, the power of the Spirit and the fact the Spirit will blow where it wishes. Can you list times when you have been guided by the Holy Spirit to actions that in hindsight were right and proper, although at the time seemed risky or contrary to the directions of others? How did it feel for you to go against the tide at that time?

The triune God

Creative

God is indeed an immense power. We know this from Exodus 33:20 when God says, 'You cannot see my face; for no one shall see me and live.' It is not just about seeing God. It is also about understanding the nature of an unknowable God.

If our God is so incomprehensible, we need some answers for our small human frames and minds to comprehend. We have our internal guide, the Holy Spirit, to steer us. Sometimes that guidance will help us to peer out of the small box in which we keep God.

We also have Jesus Christ. Without Christ's birth and God's manifestation in a human form on the earth, we would not be able to consider getting close to such an omnipresent and omnipotent God. Jesus Christ is our bridgehead to the Godhead (John 14:6).

Christ's ministry upon earth leads us by the hand to God and the Holy Spirit guides us daily further in our lives. The Trinity provides accessibility to our creator God.

Put a tray of ice cubes, a glass bowl of cold water and a boiling kettle together on your kitchen surface. Observe their different characteristics, from scalding vapour to frozen solidity. They are so dissimilar and yet all are water. Meditate upon the sameness and differences of God the Father, the Son and the Holy Spirit. Pour the boiling water and the other two elements carefully into a large washing-up bowl. Notice, by the end of your meditation, that all are one.

Dark skies

Going out

We are often encouraged to look to nature to find God. It is common to capture the beauty and detail of God in the world by carefully observing a small flower. It is here that we can begin to see how God knows when a sparrow falls. This is the God of small things.

There is, however, a part of nature that passes us by, and that is the cosmos. The reason we do not look heavenwards is that modern-day light pollution hides our view of the night sky. The cloak of modern-day living masks the magnificence and incredibility of our universe.

I recall vividly walking home to our remote cottage on a Norfolk holiday one evening. There was a gin-clear sky. As I looked up, I was spellbound by the sparkling vista that hung overhead, a twinkling mass of God's creation, a clearly visible swathe of the Milky Way – such a thick mass of stars that they appear as a milky band.

Our forebears would have seen that vista nightly. They lived in a world where the cosmos was not masked by artificial light, so they were able to have a better connection to the real nature and majesty and grandeur of God's creation.

We can find places to see God's glory in the sky. Look out for dark spaces that exist around your location. Typical dark spaces are found by moorland, the sea and uninhabited areas away from major conurbations, as well as islands. Holidays are therefore a good time to encounter these spaces. If you are fortunate enough to have dark spaces near you, take some time to stare at the wonders of the cosmos and feel the greatness of our God's creation. If you cannot find a dark space, take a clear night with a full moon and look at the beauty and majesty of the hanging moon in our night sky. If neither is possible, do an internet search for Milky Way images. You will not get the effects of scale but will capture some of the majesty.

There is a website called Dark Sky Discovery which gives the very best dark sky locations in the UK. These are the special places where you can view the true wonders of the universe in which we live.

A window into the Trinity

Meditative

Ephesians 3: 20–21 tells us God is more than we can imagine.

We cannot dream of the capacity of our Lord. We have looked at the enormity of the universe in which we live as a mirror of our awesome creator God. We have considered his omnipresence and the nature of God as being love and spirit. We have considered the human face of God in Jesus Christ and God's ongoing presence with us through the Holy Spirit.

We have explored our images of God and our need to make him a person so that we may understand God more fully. We also make him a male. Some find imagining God as female more helpful for their images of God.

While we have tried to explore the mystery and inestimable nature and size of God, we finish with a traditional depiction of the Godhead. Find a copy of the icon produced by Andrei Rublev in the early 1400s, showing the Holy Trinity. Here is a physical representation of the Trinity.

Spend some time in contemplation with this icon. In the Orthodox tradition, an icon is viewed not as a picture but as a window between the earthly and spiritual realm. It would be easy to criticise this icon; after all, we have thought about the power of God and this icon puts God in a box, making a physical manifestation of him.

But that is not the purpose of icons. They are to be used for contemplation. Gaze through the image, use it as a window to look into the wonder and majesty of our creator God, entering into the heavenly world of mystery. Look and listen with your heart and use the stillness as the medium to listen to the heart of God – the window offers a two-way view.

Lord God, enfold me in your loving arms as I gaze through this window on to your Trinity. Reveal to me the spirit of your love for me and for this world in which you have created us. Amen

Living the beatitudes

Jean Marie Dwyer OP

The beatitudes

Introduction/meditation

Each beatitude gives us a word picture of the kinds of people we need to be to receive the kingdom of God. Living the beatitudes is not optional for our Christian life. In the beatitudes, Jesus is challenging us to reflect on what is fundamental to being his follower. The text of Matthew 5:1–12 is like a mirror in which we can see the reality of our discipleship.

The language of the beatitudes is rooted in the Old Testament spirituality of God's covenant relationship with his people. Each beatitude is rich in covenant language: justice, righteousness, steadfast love, peace, truth and mercy. These words describe attributes of God for us to reflect on and live in the context of our daily life. Thus, we fulfil our destiny as God-bearers and live a godly life.

In reflecting on the beatitudes, I was touched in a new way by the integrity that needs to exist between the words I speak and the way I live my life. The beatitudes are the gospel in embryo, the manifesto of all who wish to follow Jesus. They hold the key to holiness. We receive the promise of God's blessing in each beatitude.

You might like to prepare a special 'workshop journal' to take you through the beatitudes. You will need the text of Matthew 5:1–12 and Luke 6:17–26.

Reflect on the beatitudes in Matthew 5:1–12 and Luke 6:17–26.

In your journal, paraphrase each of the beatitudes in a way that makes them more understandable and applicable for your daily life.

Ask yourself:

- How serious am I about living the beatitudes?
- Do I consider them essential to my Christian life?
- What do the 'woes' in Luke's Gospel add to my understanding of Jesus' teaching on the beatitudes?

Record your answers.

The poor in spirit

Prayer

Matthew's Gospel speaks of the 'poor in spirit', those who have opened their hearts to God's gifts. Each beatitude depends on our being poor in spirit, experientially knowing our utter dependence on God. The world is concerned with the important and mighty; only in scripture do we find the 'poor' recognised as having dignity and significance. In Luke's Gospel, the Greek word used for 'poor' literally means 'beggars': those who have nothing. All the great masters of the spiritual life insist on the importance of an empty receptivity to the working of the Holy Spirit, who dwells in our inmost being. The stripping away of all that hinders our possession of God as the source of all our actions is a constant theme. The poor in spirit receive the kingdom of heaven. Their joy and completion is in God.

Spend time today in silent prayer. Seek to empty your heart of all the many thoughts that bombard you. Imagine a vast empty space within you that belongs only to God.

End your time with a prayer asking to become poor in spirit.

Come Holy Spirit, our comforter and wisdom guide.

Dear God, fill me with the power of your Holy Spirit.
Open my heart to desire to be truly poor in spirit
that your kingdom may be within me.

Blessed are those who mourn

Reflective

God's promise includes the comfort and strengthening of the Holy Spirit as we journey toward our completion. Mourning comes to us all: the loss of loved ones, relocation, the loss of our job or friends, a time of sickness and, for some, the poverty of ageing. God is always with us during these times. There is also the grief of nations who experience poverty, oppression, lack of freedom and death. God will be our comfort. God promises, through the prophet Isaiah, that he will wipe away every tear; mourning and sadness will be no more (Isaiah 61:3; see also Revelation 21:4).

Reflect on this beatitude. What does it mean in your life?

Record ways in which you feel you can live this beatitude. What opportunities present themselves, each day, week, or month?

How have you felt in times of sorrow or hardship? Did you feel abandoned by God? Or was God your sustaining presence during those times?

Our faith tells us God is with us always in times of darkness and light. We need only to reach out to God in trust.

Recall one such experience of seeming abandonment. Sit with the experience in silence. What would you do differently? How could God have been more a part of your experience? Did the experience strengthen your trust in the God who promises to give us strength?

Is there someone whom you can comfort? We often feel at a loss in the face of grief. Sit with someone who needs comfort. Just be with the person, perhaps holding their hand. Some grief is beyond words.

Blessed are the meek

Reflective

We often look for God in the great events of life and miss his coming in the gentle breeze, his quiet presence all about us, or in the poor, meek and humble. We live in a culture that sees creation as a commodity to be used for our purposes. Sadly, even human beings are seen as articles of trade to be used and exploited. How very different is Jesus' teaching in this third beatitude. The meek are called blessed and are linked with the possession of the earth. The meek, the disfranchised, are wealthy in God's kingdom.

The meek who inherit the earth are not timid, a word usually associated with fear. On the contrary, the meek named in the third beatitude are strong and courageous people who have chosen the attitude of meekness because of their relationship to God, who is kind and compassionate and full of love. Each beatitude in its own way is related to living a life of love and reflecting God's love to others. Meekness is a gift and a virtue, instilling within us an attitude of humble, submissive and expectant trust in God, which overflows in a loving, patient and gentle attitude towards others. Such words as submissive, unassuming, gentleness and being self-effacing seem feeble to us and connected with weakness. The scripture gives quite a different picture.

Prepare a journal page on meekness.

Do you consider yourself a meek person? Or is meekness something you have associated with weakness?

Do you understand what Jesus is asking of us when he says 'Blessed are the meek'?

Jesus said of himself, 'Learn from me; for I am gentle and humble in heart' (Matthew 11:29). The Jesus who blessed the little children and asked us to be like little children is the same Jesus who drove the money changers from the temple in his zeal for his Father's house.

Perhaps meekness is a little more complicated than we think. I like to talk about the strength of meekness. The word 'gentle' is a substitute for being meek. In a hostile situation, it takes great strength and courage to be gentle and kind with someone who is harsh or angry.

Reflect on the fact that each beatitude calls us to be like God. Meekness is a response to real situations in our life. Sometimes it could be overlooking an insult or an abrasive person without retaliating. But it can also be a gentle and courageous, but truthful, response to an unfair situation or injustice to another.

How do we respond to various situations with a gentle, patient and truthful attitude? Meekness is not cowardly.

Record your thoughts.

Pray for the gift of true meekness. Today, choose to put it into practice in multiple ways as the opportunities present themselves. Be patient with someone who irritates you.

Or, have the courage to speak in a gentle but firm way in addressing a situation that needs changing, at home or in your workplace, with someone who may not take it well.

Blessed are those who hunger and thirst for righteousness

Intercession

We have an inner impulse to seek the truth, a desire for righteousness and goodness because we are one with all people in Christ

Jesus. Righteousness is synonymous with holiness of life. The word of God is clear in showing how God is righteousness and how we are related to that. Righteousness and justice are attributes of God and emanate from God's nature. The righteous God is the model of holiness given to us in the scripture, both in the Old and New Testament. In the New Testament, Jesus calls his Father righteous. The righteous God is given to us as an example of how we are to relate to our neighbour with love, fairly and in truth. We are created in God's image and have an obligation to exercise righteousness in our daily lives. The prophet Micah gives a simple formula for living our life:

> *He has told you, O mortal, what is good; and what does the Lord require of you but to do justice, and to love kindness, and to walk humbly with your God?*
> MICAH 6:8

Prepare a journal page on righteousness.

To hunger and thirst for righteousness: these are strong words for describing an inner longing for something not yet ours. Reflect on what it means to hunger and thirst for a spiritual reality.

What are your inner spiritual hunger and thirsts? Are they in harmony with this beatitude?

What practical actions do the words of this beatitude suggest to you? What do they mean for so many people who thirst for justice and righteousness? What can you do?

Hunger and thirst for justice and righteousness have very real dimensions for so many people in our world who are not free, who know oppression, violence and hatred. This beatitude speaks to this reality also.

Take time today to listen to the world news. Pray specifically for so many who are suffering displacement, violence and death. Focus on one person, known to God, and spend your day praying for him or her. Our prayers should focus not only on the victims but on those who are perpetrating violence, division and hate in our world.

Blessed are the merciful

Action

A search for loving unity among all peoples is the healing answer for a new world that is free from violence and war: a society where the innate dignity of every human person is recognised. Such a beautiful new world begins by the recognition of our responsibility to love, and our concrete choices to put love into practice. God calls us to the practice of love for all those who touch our life each day. In doing this, we begin building a new world. Our witness reverberates to others and gives expression to our power to effect changes step by step.

Mercy is an indispensable virtue for loving. Mercy and love are attributed to the work of the Holy Spirit within us. Mercy is not a generic term; mercy always has a human face. It is the face of each person I will meet this day.

Prepare a journal page on the gift of mercy.

God promises us that the merciful will receive mercy – something to reflect upon and take very seriously. It is comparable to Jesus' words in the Lord's Prayer: if we forgive, we will be forgiven. This is serious for our Christian life.

To be merciful, it is necessary to see the needs of others in the light of love, and with belief in their good intentions. Give the benefit of the doubt to someone who treats you harshly today. Perhaps they are not feeling well or are troubled. Reciprocate with mercy.

Extend mercy to those who need your forgiveness, today.

Is there someone in your life whom you need to love more in

tender mercy. Our response to others depends on our relationship to a loving and merciful God, and not on their perfection.

Blessed are the pure in heart

Creative

Who are the pure in heart who will see God? They are those who are empty, free, detached, open to the Holy Spirit and utterly dependent on God's grace working in, and through, them. The pure in heart listen to the voice of the Spirit and obey with joy. Purity of heart consists in the habitual state of our inner spirit from which our actions will flow.

The early monks of the desert sought purity of heart as the goal of their lives at the time, and as the final fulfilment of their blessedness in heaven. It is by purity of heart, Jesus tells us, that we shall see God, even in this life dimly, and in all fullness in eternity.

Our work is to open our hearts to receive this gift from God. To be pure in heart is not something we can achieve on our own. Yet, it is a gift that God so desires to pour into our hearts through the Holy Spirit.

Purity of heart is the gift that restores grace to our heart and gives us the capacity to see God. This gift is God's way of preparing us to live in his presence eternally.

Our work is to prepare our hearts for this gift by our surrender to the Holy Spirit through our daily commitment to live Jesus' teaching: by detaching ourselves little by little from all that is not God.

In your journal, write in your own words what you believe purity of heart will mean in your life. Let the above thoughts guide you.

List a plan for seeking purity of heart every day. What practical things can you do? What can you do to remind yourself of this plan?

Above all, every day, pray sincerely to receive the gift of purity of heart and follow the guidance of the Holy Spirit.

Blessed are the peacemakers

Going out

Peace is what our world is constantly seeking; it often seems to be such an elusive gift. True and lasting peace is a gift of God. In the Old Testament, perfect peace was linked to doing God's will and faithfulness to the covenant. Jesus speaks of it when he tells the apostles that the peace he is giving them is not the peace the world gives. The peace that God gives resides in our inmost being, even amid turmoil and suffering. Only in the harmony of being toward God and united with one another in love can the world achieve peace. The reign of God will bring the fullness of peace. We begin to taste God's peace in this life, but it is only in eternal life that all discord will cease because the knowledge of God will fill all things. Our world is in such need of peacemakers. Becoming a peacemaker in our environment and among those we touch each day helps to transform the world.

In this beatitude, being peacemakers relates to being children of God. Jesus' teaching on becoming like a little child is one of the hardest sayings of the gospel to fulfil, especially in our modern culture. Our sophisticated society lives by appearances. The appearance of maturity, of success, of control and of power. So often we are not real, but only embracing an illusion to impress others with our importance and status.

Paradoxically, it takes mature decisions to become like a little child.

Watch a little child playing, discovering a pretty pebble or some other simple thing. There is such delight, an intense focus on a small particle of creation. Sadly, in our Western culture, even our children are losing their childhood and their sense of wonder.

Our world is in such need of peacemakers. Becoming a peacemaker in our environment and among those we touch each day helps to transform the world. Opening our hearts to the gentle flow of the Holy Spirit fills us with peace that we, in turn, can share with those around us. God is willing to give us gifts abundantly. God's gifts transform us and, through us, transform the world. So spend some time in simple wonder at a small thing. Go for a walk and look out for beautiful things. When you find one, pause and spend time enjoying it, wondering at its beauty and the one who created it.

Blessed are those who are persecuted for righteousness' sake

Reflective

We do not find life challenging in the good experiences of life; rather, it is in the times of need and adversity we seek God more intensely.

A young woman in her 30s once told me that she was an atheist because she had never felt the need for God. There had not been any traumatic experiences in her life or situations that she had not been able to handle by herself. Yet God is not only with us for times of calamity; God walks with us in all the circumstances of our life.

What is this beatitude all about? Probably, when you reflect on it, the first thing that comes to mind is the martyrs who suffered persecution and death as disciples of Jesus. Each beatitude offers a special challenge to a deeper way of living discipleship. The challenge of the tenth beatitude is about Christian witness and being counter-cultural in the daily events of our life. Jesus is asking us to exercise our Christian vocation as prophets.

Prepare a journal page for the mystery of persecution that comes into our lives by being faithful Christians.

Reflect on the story above. What does it teach you? Record your thoughts.

Perhaps if we are always comfortable and without challenges in living our faith, we are missing something?

This beatitude is about finding God in the daily events of our life, especially in times of misunderstanding, and adversity. Think back on the last 24 hours. Imagine the video playing your life in the past day. Invite God to watch it with you, and to show you where he was present and what he was doing.

Blessed are you when people revile you

Action

If we give witness to the Christian values – love, kindness, honesty, fair-dealing – choose not to climb the corporate ladder at the expense of others and recognise the dignity of each person with whom we daily deal, we are very likely to experience 'persecution'. We will stand out as different, and a little odd. It is hard to live the truth in the face of the expectations of our culture and those around us. The world will isolate us and try to eradicate what sets a standard of judgement against their way of living. Often, we do not want to rock the social boat. We want to fit in and to be popular. Jesus asks something more of us, to live the gospel and allow God's love and mercy to be reflected through us.

Prepare a journal page for this beatitude. Is there someone in your life who is jealous of you or envies your gifts? This can be a very painful situation. Jesus tells us not to hide our light or the light of the gospel under a bushel basket. We need to reject the fear of being different if it prevents us from allowing God's light to shine through us to others.

Do an act of kindness to a friend or someone in the workplace without worrying about what others think.

Rejoice and be glad

Going out

Jesus ends his sermon in Matthew's Gospel by telling us to rejoice when we are reviled, persecuted and suffer as Jesus' followers. Is that possible? Yes, when we allow the joy of the Holy Spirit to flow through us and we forget ourselves and keep our spiritual gaze fixed on Jesus.

God is found in the peace of hearts that are given to him: a peace beyond understanding that, in a ripple effect, radiates out, even now, into the world. The kingdom of God is already among us. The good news of the gospel is that we will be satisfied.

In your journal, make a list of the ways God has blessed you.

Go out and find some still water (or use a large bowl at home). Throw a stone into the water and watch the ripples spreading out and reaching the edge. As you watch, allow God's peace to spread through you, rippling to the edges of your being.

Write a reflection on the beauty of this beatitude, God's promises and how God has fulfilled them in your life.

Eyes to see and ears to hear

Reflective

In striving to live the beatitudes, I am daily reminded of my solidarity with all my brothers and sisters. For the beatitudes call me to be poor, empty and dependent on God, to mourn with the grieving, to hunger and thirst for justice, to be merciful, to embrace the strength of meekness and to be a person of peace. These are certainly all qualities needed in our world today. When we live these beautiful Gospel qualities, we are transforming the small corner of the world in which we live.

Jesus' teaching in the beatitudes turns the wisdom of the world upside down. The world is concerned with the important and mighty; in the scriptures, the 'poor' are elevated and recognised as having worth and dignity. The beatitudes address the human condition in a broken world where so many suffer and go unrecognised; Jesus' promises in the beatitudes say loud and clear that their suffering is seen by a loving God.

How do we see life? Our attitude to the things arounds us, and our encounter with others, makes a great difference to our perspective of life.

When I walked in the woods with a friend of mine, although we both saw the same landscape, our experience of the creation about us was so dissimilar. The difference came from our attitudes, the vision of the heart. I would see the beauty of the trees and the blue of the sky, the singing birds and scampering squirrels. She would see the broken branches and rotten wood: the disorder and brokenness. To be real, we need both views. It is necessary to perceive the brokenness in our world, and in ourselves, to heal it. Yet, that can never be enough without seeing beyond the brokenness to the beauty.

How do you believe that the beatitudes show you God's plan of restoration in our broken world?

How can living the beatitudes heal and transform your life?

Do you have a plan for living each beatitude in a new way?

Journeying with the Psalms

Lynne Chitty

Journeying with the Psalms

Introduction

Life is full of journeys. Some are life-changing, tedious, challenging, painful, exhilarating or short. One is lifelong.

We journey with many different companions too. Some are by our side most of the way. Some we encounter briefly. Some are flesh and blood. Others are moods and feelings, health or sicknesses. Sometimes we journey in great numbers; often we journey alone.

The Psalms, all 150 of them, have something profound and real to say to us as we journey. Some are to be sung along the way. Some will speak into the depths of our fears. Some are like a hand to hold and some are as a silent companion when words are beyond us.

They are steeped in history. Jesus would have known them from childhood, and they are still set to music today in fresh ways and in celebration of their riches. Psalms like Psalm 23 still accompany many on their last journey and continue to bring strength and courage to those left behind.

That said, they are not always an easy read or all sweetness and light. They are about the human condition in all its strength and all its frailty. It is for that reason they are still so relevant.

St Benedict made the Psalms an integral part of his Rule of Life. All the Psalms were read or sung each week. The monks encountered the range of despairing, doubtful, bitter, vindictive, self-pitying, nationalistic and angry voices in the Psalter. It is not that every sentiment is admirable, but that in praying the Psalms we confront ourselves as we really are. The Psalms are a reality check to keep prayer from becoming sentimental, superficial or detached from the real world, which is full of real people struggling with their relationship with God, with one another and with their own limitations.

The monks would have known the Psalms by heart. You can start your journey with the Psalms by learning one today.

Psalm 117 is the shortest psalm and makes a beautiful prayer of affirmation, and praise. Try making up a tune so you can sing the psalm.

Praise the Lord, all you nations! Extol him, all you peoples! For great is his steadfast love towards us, and the faithfulness of the Lord endures for ever. Praise the Lord!

Psalm 1

Creative

'Let's start at the very beginning. A very good place to start.' These words from *The Sound of Music* apply very well to the Psalms. The first three verses of Psalm 1 are a gateway through which we go as we begin our journey. They give us a vital piece of advice essential to take with us: use a map. This map is the law of the Lord, which is the whole of scripture. 'Happy,' says the psalmist, 'are those who meditate on the law of the Lord.' To delight in the law is not just to look at the scenery as we journey, but to take it deep within us and tuck it away to bring out when life throws up challenges and disappointments and opportunities. If we do that, then our journey will be fruitful, we will bear fruit in due season. We will have a deep stability and rootedness in God which is as secure as the roots of a tree.

Read the first three verses again and draw a picture of a tree with the roots showing. Under the roots, write words that symbolise where you find your security. On the branches, write where you feel your life is fruitful. On the ground, draw a few leaves that have fallen from your tree. Pray about each one – the ones that you have been glad to let go and the ones you grieve for.

Loving God, to delight in your word is to be blessed with rich nourishment for life's journey. May I draw closer to you as I read your psalms and embrace your will for my life. Amen

Psalm 16

Reflective

The opening verses of this song are both a prayer for protection and an affirmation of trust. It speaks too of inheritance, which the psalmist enjoys now as he celebrates the sense of God being at his right hand, but which is ultimately an eternal inheritance. God's faithfulness is for now and it is for eternity. The psalmist declares that God is all he has and he celebrates that God is more than enough. His fears are overridden by his belief that God will show him the path of life and he trusts that the path will lead to the kingdom of heaven. If God wants our greatest good, then we can breathe a huge sigh of relief – we cannot get lost on the journey and we cannot lose the inheritance that Jesus died to bless us with.

Gather on a table (or imagine gathering) some things that you have inherited in your life and things that you would like to leave to others. Spend time enjoying them all.

Pray too for those whose faith you have inherited and for those you would most like to pass your faith on to. Be aware of the receiving and the passing on of both possessions and faith.

Psalm 18

Creative

> *I love you, O Lord, my strength… my rock in whom I take refuge.*
> PSALM 18:1–2

Refuge is a big word in the Psalms. God is repeatedly called a refuge. This is the only support that we can ultimately rely on when storms hit our journey, when we are exhausted, alone, demoralised or afraid. In Psalm 2, David took refuge in remembering that God would ultimately put things right. In Psalm 7, he took refuge in resting in God's wisdom for the plan of his life.

In Psalm 18, David's refuge is in remembering and thanking God for past blessings, and remembering the times he has been brought safely through another close encounter that has threatened his life. The word he uses for 'love' in the opening line is an unusual Hebrew word that conveys deep emotion and passion. David bares his heart and soul as he declares his love for his God. He doesn't withhold any part of himself. Every bit of who he is loves every bit of the God who has saved and blessed him.

Whether you are crying out today for God to be your refuge or whether you are singing 'I love you, O Lord', write your own psalm that expresses how you feel. It may only be one or two lines, or it may be a long heartfelt pouring out of all you have kept inside. Be real. Be honest. Be reassured that God hears all you say and all that you cannot find words for.

Psalm 22

Creative/intercession

If we were beginning to feel rather comfortable about the Psalms, the words of this psalm bring us back to the reality of suffering. It is especially poignant because it contains Christ's words from the cross, so it is impossible to read the psalm without reliving the events of Good Friday and feeling something of the agony and horror of the most hideous of deaths – crucifixion.

And yet... it ends on a note of hope, promise, salvation and redemption. 'God has done it,' cries David. 'It is finished,' cries Jesus on the cross. God has stayed by his suffering Son and his death wasn't futile. God is, was and will always be alongside those in pain, bringing some good out of even the most desperate situations. It is hard to hang on to that. It is impossible to see sometimes and it doesn't diminish pain or suffering one iota. It can, though, somewhere deep within us, save us from ultimate despair. God is at the beginning of our journey as we set out, and he is at the end. He is with us through every dark night and every morning when the effort to get up is just too much. There is a spark of hope in that and that hope is resurrection.

Cut out stories from the newspaper of situations where God seems absent. Light a candle and pray the light of hope into the lives and places before you. Pray too for the light of hope in the places where you are hurting.

Psalms 42–43

Going out

I always think of these as the see-saw psalms. The psalmist is in the depths of despair, but doesn't really know why. Then, for no apparent reason, he is upbeat again, trusting in God's love and plans and rejoicing in God's presence. He starts with a deep, deep longing for the waters that will quench his unbearable thirst. He remembers happier times and comes to the dreadful conclusion that God has forgotten him. His see-saw is at its lowest. Then, gradually, the water he craves begins to trickle and he gently laps up the realisation that God is still there within reach. He trusts he will bounce back, his see-saw will rise high again and life will be balanced; he trusts his journey will resume and his wellbeing will be restored.

We all have days where, for no reason, we wake up low. The list of things we have to do is beyond our strength, or the emptiness of the day is just too much. We suddenly notice and feel that nothing at all is right with our lives. It's not self-pity; it is a mood that can overwhelm and threaten to rob us of all we thought was good and worth living for. Equally, we can wake up singing, with a spring in our step and thinking life is just the best. Mostly, we live somewhere in the middle, but it is good to know that we are not alone in our moods. The psalmist has been there and left us a precious mark on our map.

If it is at all possible and you have a park near you, go and play on a see-saw (with a friend). Eyebrows may be raised, but be brave! Feel the ups and the downs as you play, the highs and the lows. If you are on your own, you could try a swing instead for the same feeling of high and low. If the park isn't possible, stand tall and then bend down. Give thanks for something good in your life as you stand up and entrust to God something that drags you down when you crouch. If you aren't so mobile, simply close your eyes and imagine yourself doing it as you pray.

Psalm 61

Going out

God as a refuge recurs in this psalm, but the verse I love the most is the call to 'lead me to the rock that is higher than I' (v. 2). So many times that verse has been my prayer when I have been stuck in the rut of my littleness and my limitations, and I have longed to be lifted above the difficulties of life and set on a rock where no problems could reach me and I could be protected from the assaults of the world for a while.

Of course, wherever we go we take all we are with us, but a high place gives us a different perspective and our prayer is that it will be God's perspective. Looking at our lives – where we have come from, where we might be heading – from a perspective bigger than our own can be life-changing. In small ways, drawing us out of our self-pity, or despair at how hopeless everything is. In big ways, because from higher up we can see further, and with God's perspective we can see with God's heart and God's love. Go to an upper window, or go out to the top of a hill and, when you are ready, pray.

God of all the world, vast and tiny, set me on a rock that is higher than I and grant me to see through your eyes, to listen with your ears, to rest in your strength and, when the moment comes, to act with the love of your heart. Amen

Psalm 81

Creative

When we think of commandments, they are usually big asks, so this psalm can come as a surprise as we are commanded to be joyful – to sing and to make music! Joy isn't the same as happiness and it isn't something we can pretend or conjure up, but it is a response, like gratitude, that is tucked away in our hearts and which we can draw on and release as we look to God and away from ourselves.

Verses 8–10 echo Exodus 20:2, which immediately precedes the giving of the ten commandments. In the psalm, however, just when we think there might be more dos and don'ts, God surprises us again – reassuring us, reminding us of his love and promising to feed us. We don't have to think of commandments as negative and we can see God's wisdom immersed in them. To be obedient needn't mean struggle; it can mean joy.

Try expressing joy today. You might be able to play a musical instrument, or you could sing your favourite hymn or song, or listen to recorded or live music. In your own way – 'Sing aloud to God your strength and shout for joy.'

Singing on a long journey can make the time go much quicker and help us forget how tired we are or how much we ache!

Psalm 91

Reflective

In the opening verses, the psalmist uses two contrasting images for God as our protector. A fortress and a feathered wing couldn't be more different. One sounds splendidly solid, the other unbelievably vulnerable. The thick stone walls of the fortress stop all spears and arrows. The covering wings of a mother bird are fragile and she only protects her young by bearing the cold and the dangers herself.

How can God be both? In Jesus we have a clue to the answer: he is both the King of kings and the lamb. He conquers death, but only by suffering and dying. It is his wounded hands that heal. The end of the psalm promises that if we put our trust in him, the strength and the vulnerability of God will be his gift to us in trouble. It won't save us from trouble and our journey won't be all plain sailing, but it will be blessed with and surrounded by the love of God.

Light a candle and give thanks and pray for all those who have supported you in your journey of life so far, those whose strength has been an inspiration and those whose vulnerability has been their gift.

Psalm 137

Creative

Psalm 137 is one of the most moving and heartfelt psalms as we look around the world and see refugees weeping. Hundreds of miles from home, their countries and communities being torn apart and their families living in conditions that make for tears not music.

It is also one of the most brutal psalms if we read it to the end, but the longing for revenge and retribution are real; they were real then and they are real now.

Praying for victims and aggressors can be a hard calling. Seeing the faces or worse, the bodies, of children on our TV screens can make us angry and desperate to see an end to violence. We try to balance justice and retaliation, but trying to be peacemakers not warmongers is hard. We are called to pray, even as our hearts are breaking and we have hate in our hearts. Try praying using all your emotions. We dishonour those we pray for if we give any less.

Watch the news and, as you do so, write down in different coloured pencils or paints the words that describe how you feel. If you can't find any words, don't be afraid to leave the paper blank and just write on it the places most on your heart, or use the colours before you to express yourself.

God of all the places of violence, abandoned homes and broken families, we bring to you the best and the worst of our emotions and feelings and ask that you would make of them your prayer for your world and all who suffer in it. Amen

Psalm 139

Creative

According to the psalmist, God knit us together in our mother's womb and knows us inside out and through and through. Every thought that flits through our minds, every dream we cherish and choice we make, every step of our journey that we take, our past, our present and our future; all are held in God's hands and are known in God's heart.

This can be both comforting and disconcerting, but is always beyond our understanding. This is a psalm of ownership. We are God's children; we always have been and we always will be. As we near the end of our journey, this psalm enables us to look back and see how God has journeyed with us, even when we felt alone. It allows us to look ahead too and trust that whatever lies over the next hill, or around the next bend, we will not have to face it without the love and grace and strength of our creator and guide.

If you can knit, try knitting a square and, as you knit, make each row a prayer. Starting from childhood to today, pray over each stage of your life, including both the good and the bad. When you have completed the square, keep it with you as a reminder of all you have come through and all you have enjoyed. Then knit a second square with each row a hope for the future – for you, your family and friends. If you can't knit, you could learn or you could find some play bricks and build a wall to illustrate your past and your hopes for the future.

Psalm 150

Creative

Like every good concert or firework display, the best psalm is saved to last and the collection ends with a great explosion of celebration and praise! It is right that the last psalm is about praise because, if we truly share every step of our way with God, in the end we will always be full of thankfulness and gratitude. All roads lead to that place and all hearts in the end find their fullest joy in praise and thankfulness. The last line, 'Let everything that has breath praise the Lord' (v. 6), is a prayer to carry in your heart each morning and each night. It is a prayer that can lift our spirits as we imagine all creation praising its creator. What a world that would be.

Create a collage of creation praising God. Cut out pictures or paint or draw them. Use the completed picture as your prayer and allow the last line of the last psalm to speak to you, to bring you hope and to inspire you.

As you continue your journey, allow the psalms to be a companion and draw you closer to God. They might have been written a long time ago, but they have spoken afresh to each generation since and they are living words for us today.

Small things

Karen Herrick

Small wonder!

Introduction

The Bible is full of small wonders: instances where God uses people or things that seem insignificant to achieve mighty things to further his kingdom.

In Zechariah 4:6–10, a new temple is being built by Zerubbabel to replace the one erected by Solomon and destroyed by the Babylonians. It is not as grand as the previous one, and those who can remember the splendour of the previous temple are unhappy. God's word comes to Zechariah reminding the people not to despise 'the day of small things' (v. 10). They are not to know, but this temple will be the one wherein God's Son, Jesus, will walk and teach. As God's people, we are still being asked to trust in the unseen – 'not by might nor by power, but by my Spirit' (v. 6) – that, despite our misgivings, God knows the future and has all in hand.

So often, we bemoan the small and insignificant in our lives, failing to realise their full potential or see them with God's eyes, looking at the smallness of now, rather than to the transformational power of God's Spirit.

I wonder what small things there are in your life that have the potential for greatness, if you surrender them to God and allow him to nurture them into being. Consider whether there might be a 'small thing' in your life that you have previously overlooked or considered not good enough. Are you able to give this to God and trust him for the outcome? Often, we don't see the larger effect of smaller actions, as they ripple across other people's lives.

Fill a bowl with water, letting it become still and calm, then touch your finger gently on to the surface, watching the action of that one small act ripple outwards. Trust God today that he can use small things in your life to achieve great things in his kingdom.

Small words... big difference

Creative

Read Luke 17:11–19. Jesus heals ten lepers, yet only one returns to thank him. All ten had faith enough to follow Jesus' instructions to go show themselves to the priest, expecting healing from their request for Jesus to show them pity – and receiving it. Jesus did far more than they asked. He showed that he knew their deepest longing for healing, acting with compassion to provide it and revealing himself as God's Son, healer and miracle worker.

Despite this great gift, only *one* came back to thank Jesus. Neither did he come back quietly, muttering polite gratitude. He 'came back, praising God in a loud voice' (v. 15), throwing himself at Jesus' feet, seemingly keen to share his gratefulness to Jesus with everyone. In that act, he received another gift – that of encountering Jesus for the second time, acknowledging the difference that he had made in his life.

Most of us will not have received miraculous physical healing like this, but each of us has so much to be grateful for. Today, as you go through the day, try to intentionally recall every blessing you encounter... from the smallest thing to larger mercies. As you name these blessings, firstly, thank God for each of them – out loud if you dare! Secondly, try to share your gratitude with at least one other person today. Thirdly, make a conscious effort to say thank you to people around you, in response to what they do for you. 'Thank you' is such a small thing to say, but expressing our gratitude can make a big difference in our own lives and attitude and the lives of others.

A small boy with great faith

Creative

Read 1 Samuel 17:1–50. This is such a well-known story, and yet I never fail to be captivated by its narrative. Here we have a stand-off between God's people, the Israelites, on one side of the valley, with the Philistines on the other, each waiting for the other to strike – for the army that did would incur great casualties and likely lose the battle. In the meantime, Goliath the Philistine champion goads the Israelites with his defiance.

Enter David the shepherd boy, come to bring provisions for his brothers on the front line. On hearing Goliath's taunts, David is incensed that anyone can 'defy the armies of the living God' (v. 26) and offers to fight. He is dismissed as useless against one as experienced as Goliath. But David is insistent, confident in his God-given abilities, honed in different circumstances as a lone shepherd protecting the sheep from wild animals. Equipped only with the familiar staff, sling and stones he has spent many years mastering, David goes out, not in his own strength but in God's, knowing that the battle belongs to him. It is this trust that makes the difference, allowing the Israelite army to triumph against such odds.

David was faithful in serving God where he was put. He was a good shepherd, accepting his role and mastering skills with the tools that he was given, to do a menial job well. God honoured this commitment by using him for a much bigger task. Sometimes we can find ourselves in places not of our choosing, but it is important to remember that we can serve God wherever we are. We do not know how God may use the seemingly insignificant in the future.

Find five small stones and place them somewhere you will see them regularly, to reflect. Perhaps place them in the shape of a cross or other significant shape, as a reminder that God can use each one of us powerfully, no matter how insignificant we may feel, if we commit our ways to him and trust in his almighty power.

Small actions and distractions

Intercession

I wonder how you deal with distractions. Often, we can be less than Christ-like when interrupted from our seemingly important business. Head down, we plough ahead, failing to check in with God about how he would have us act. Pause to consider your own reactions when you are distracted from a task in hand. Ask for forgiveness if you feel the need.

Jesus was often interrupted while he was about God's business, but he was never distracted from it. He acted with insight through being close to his Father, exercising understanding, compassion and grace to all who approached him. In Matthew 9:18–25, Jesus was teaching his disciples when asked to raise the ruler's daughter from the dead, but he did not respond by saying 'Go away, I'm busy teaching' or, 'Sorry, there's nothing more to be done'. Instead, he got up and went with the father, responding immediately to the need in hand. So, when Jesus is interrupted again by a woman touching the hem of his garment trusting in faith to be healed, it could have been easy to ignore such a small gesture. But Jesus recognises when a small gesture is the culmination of huge effort and faith, and responds with affirmation and healing.

The challenge is for us too, to recognise where God may be working through the small distractions in our own lives. Can we be so in tune with God that we can bring God-light into these encounters?

Today, use any distractions you encounter as an opportunity to draw close to God, praying that you might act as Jesus would. Perhaps you could hold the hem of your garment as you pray for the situation you are in, remembering both the woman's faith and Jesus' response to this small action.

Small and narrow

Imaginative

Gates are usually outside, controlling the comings and goings of people or animals. The broader the gate, the easier it is for many people at a time to travel from one place to another. With a wider gate, there is easier access, and the possibility of getting caught up in a crowd to drift through a gate, perhaps unaware of our transition from one place to another. A narrow gate tends to restrict travellers to smaller numbers, often ensuring that only one can pass through at a time. Anyone entering a narrow gate will often be away from the beaten track and probably need to make a conscious decision to lift the latch or climb the stile. The traveller may need to unload any baggage they carry to squeeze through an opening.

Imagine yourself in front of a narrow gate. Take time to picture in detail what you are wearing and carrying, physically and emotionally. Look at the gate and see it in detail, noting its age, appearance and colour; its setting… Where is it? In an urban or rural setting? How did you find it? Where does it lead to? What time of day is it? Look for the latch on the gate. Consider your feelings as you approach. Are you keen to enter, nervous, reluctant, excited or something else? Try not to judge yourself but accept whatever feelings come as the scenario unfolds in your imagination. Talk to God about whatever it is you have imagined, listening to him and reflecting on your response.

Read Matthew 7:13–14 and John 10:9. How do these verses speak to you in the light of your imaginary journey through the narrow gate? How do you feel about being one of the few who find Jesus the gate? Do you feel the safety, freedom and pasture that Jesus promises in John 10:9? This week, perhaps you can be especially aware of your comings and goings and, as you come across gates or doors in your daily living, think more on your approach to the narrow gate.

Faith as small as a mustard seed

Creative

Seeds are no small things. Hold a fruit seed in your hand, considering its potential for growth. Unless we knew, how could we possibly imagine that such an unassuming object could hold such latent possibility? Seeds remain dormant, waiting to awaken into life. They need planting, watering and nurturing into growth. Something that looks so lifeless has, given the right opportunities, the ability to grow, flourish, bloom and fruit – producing over the years an infinite number of seeds that touch many lives across many continents.

Reflect on your own potential for growth, particularly regarding your faith, drawing sustenance from the fact that even a small amount of faith can move seemingly insurmountable problems (see Matthew 17:20–21). What would make your faith grow? What do you need to grow spiritually? What lessons can you learn for what God is awakening and germinating in you? Remember 'It's not the one who plants or the one who waters who is at the centre of this process, but God, who makes things grow' (1 Corinthians 3:7, MSG).

Seeds often take a long time to grow into established healthy plants. So too with us. Faith takes time to grow and mature, as we experience the nurturing, but sometimes painful pruning hand of our Father the gardener (John 15:1–4).

Plant some seeds this week. Take time to reflect as you nurture them into growth, identifying aspects that may help your own spiritual growth, waiting on God to help you grow your small faith into one that can move mountains, giving all the glory to him.

Obedience in small things

Liturgy

Read 2 Kings 5:1–19.

Sometimes we look to God for complex solutions, too proud to acknowledge that the answer is closer to hand and much simpler than we were expecting. Naaman was a reputable military commander of the king, courageous and wealthy, yet afflicted by the then-incurable disease of leprosy. Still, he was not above following advice from his servants and, in laying aside his pride, he came to know God.

It was his young Israelite slave girl who knew God's healing power through the prophet Elisha, and was bold enough to suggest a way forward. Perhaps we can reflect on how her small voice ultimately brought Naaman to faith, daring to trust that this could happen to people we know when we use our small voice to tell of God's goodness and power. I wonder how many times we have held back in speaking out, thinking that our God is too small to act?

Washing seven times in the Jordan is not the way that Naaman envisioned his healing. He is angry with Elisha, who doesn't even deign to meet him, and furious at the suggestion to wash in the Jordan, which is small and dirty compared to the rivers in his own country. Yet again, it is his servants who speak out, encouraging humility and obedience as a pathway to potential healing. Think of how this speaks into your own life, reflecting on how we can learn by listening to others, putting aside pride and acting in godly humility and obedience, even when we do not understand.

Can we see how this story echoes our own baptism, as we are washed clean from our sins? Use a bowl of water to renew your baptism vows, slowly scooping water into your hands seven times as you say the following phrases:

1 You are my God and I will worship you.
2 I will follow Jesus as my guide.
3 Help me to stand firm against evil.
4 Forgive me and wash me clean when I fail.
5 May my life tell of the good news of Jesus.
6 May I serve others and seek justice.
7 May I live in humble obedience to God.

Small coins of great sacrifice

Visual

Read Mark 12:41–44. Now take two pennies (or the two lowest value of coins that you have) and hold them in the palm of your hand. Think of the woman's gift to the temple treasury and the reaction of Jesus. She 'out of her poverty, put in everything – all she had to live on' (v. 44). In today's currency, her coins would equate to around 1/64th of a day's wage. I wonder what amount that represents for you. Would this be all you had to live on? Using these two coins (or replacing them with coins more relevant to you), carry them with you for the day or place them somewhere you will pass by regularly. Whenever you hold them or see them, spend some time with God asking what this story might mean to you today.

What change in your giving might it effect, noting that giving can encompass many things? Perhaps God may be nudging you to respond in some way that involves the generous and sacrificial giving of your time, energy, knowledge, patience, support or something else? Remember, too, that our attitude to giving is key to its worth in God's eyes and can be part of our gratefulness for all that he has given us.

Perhaps use this mnemonic throughout the week if it helps:

Give generously,
In love,
Freely,
Trusting God for the future.

It's a small world

Going out

Go for a slow, steady walk outside, taking in the wonder of creation. Breathe in its goodness and healing power and give thanks. Look especially at the small things that our God has created: a blade of grass, small flower, leaf, feather, worm, ant, stone... There is so much to choose from. Spend time with each thing you are drawn to, touching or holding it, looking carefully, giving thanks and wondering. Listen for all God may be teaching you from each thing. For example: consider how the smoothness and patterns of a stone reveal the narrative of the past. Imagine it splitting from rocks; the friction from turbulent waters that has broken it, worn it down and shaped it. What does this say to me? Can I trust that the stormy times of my life and the hard things that wear me down are, in fact, acting as a catalyst, shaping and refining me to be a better person? Choose other natural things to reflect upon if you have time.

Refer to Proverbs 30:24–28 and see how the writer used this method to reflect on four small creatures. What features in them can you identify that provide wisdom for your own life?

Receiving like a small child

Creative

In Luke 18:15–17, Jesus tells his disciples that 'anyone who will not receive the kingdom of God like a little child will never enter it' (v. 17). Why is this? What character traits does a young child have that enables them to freely receive from God?

Ponder on this as you recall to mind any young children you know. Write down as many of their attributes as you can think of and then compare them to your own. Is there one particular trait lacking in yourself that saddens you? Or perhaps you still retain many child-like characteristics? 'Jesus called the children to him' (v. 16), just as he calls each one of us. Go to him now. Answer his call. Spend time sharing how you feel.

Young children are full of life, energy and wonder about their world. They are trusting, honest, kind, resilient and open to change. They are very persistent, and often brave, full of endless questions. Use this list as well as your own to help you as you talk with your Lord. To consolidate, try to spend some time with a young child this week in a simple playful activity like blowing bubbles, playing ball or colouring. Continue to allow the passage to speak to you as you share with and learn from them. If this is not possible, then buy a pot of bubbles, go outside and use them to play as you pray.

Small spark

Reflective

We each have the potential to build each other up or tear down. What we say can encourage or dishearten, lift the spirits or wound and hurt. Words can act like bullets, staying embedded in our minds for many years, affecting our self-belief and actions, or they can be like a blanket providing comfort, reconciliation and restoration.

Bring before God now any words that may have caused past hurt and ask him to bring about healing. Give thanks for positive words that have helped you through your life's journey. Read James 3:5–12 and then reflect on these verses from *The Message*: 'A word out of your mouth may seem of no account, but it can accomplish nearly anything – or destroy it! It only takes a spark, remember, to set off a forest fire. A careless or wrongly placed word out of your mouth can do that. By our speech we can ruin the world, turn harmony to chaos, throw mud on a reputation...' (James 3:4–6), followed by words from Psalm 19:14: 'May these words of my mouth and this meditation of my heart be pleasing in your sight, Lord, my Rock and my Redeemer.'

Pray these words for yourself, using actions – gently touching your mouth and then your heart with both hands, then making your hands into a rock shape and stretching them to a cross. Or perhaps write a prayer or poem, expressing your feelings about the power of words and asking God to guard your words so that they become a source of good.

Seeing the big picture

Going out/creative

In the Bible, as in life, it is often the seemingly small and apparently insignificant things that turn out to be the most important; the pixels that create the bigger picture. So, to end the series, we will creatively consider five small words in the Bible that could so easily be glossed over: 'He also made the stars' (Genesis 1:16).

Go out and spend some time looking at the night sky. Take in the enormity of space and time, the attention of our creator God to detail, the unfathomable infinity of space... and praise God. Now, spend ten minutes finding out as much as you can about stars, or go back to the section on 'The greatness of God – how big is God?' (p. 32) and remind yourself of the hugeness of the universe. Did you know that there are over 200 million within the Milky Way alone? That light from stars takes millions of years to reach earth, so when we look up at the sky we are in effect, looking back in time? Or that the colour of stars is dictated by how hot they are, ranging from brown to blue?

Using a plain piece of paper and coloured pencil crayons, felt-tip pens or paints, write in the centre of the page the verse from Genesis, 'He also made the stars.' (Or use the page in your Bible if you like.) Now, using media of your choice, draw stars of different sizes, shapes and colours around the page. Add words of praise as you create, using the time to think of the enormity of our God, the star-maker and God of small things.

Lost in translation

Joy McCormick

Different languages

Introduction

Anyone who has learned a second language knows the frustration which often arises in trying to make an accurate translation. Choices must be made between possible alternative meanings of a word, significant ambiguities, word plays, cultural nuances, poetic rhythm and rhyme. These are just some features lost in translation. The richness of the original language often fails to survive. How much, then, has been lost to us as our scriptures have passed from oral Aramaic to written Greek, then through scholarly Latin to English?

Of course, language is not the only form of translation which must be considered. There is also translation from the culture of origin to another with quite different values and world view. To offer a simple example from my New Zealand culture – the Maori word *whenua* is usually translated 'land' (as in *Tangata whenua* – 'people of the land'). However, *whenua* is also the word for the placenta, and knowing this explains the Maori attitude to their tribal land which continues to nourish and shape them as the placenta did before birth. Far from being valued according to what can be extracted from it (whether produce or minerals), or as a commodity to be traded or sold, it is their very identity. All this is lost in the purely verbal translation – 'land'.

Then there is the issue of translation across time – from the prescientific era to the 21st century; from a three-tier, earth-centred universe to modern understandings of the cosmos.

I am no scholar of ancient biblical languages, so must rely on the work of others such as Neil Douglas-Klotz (*The Hidden Gospel* et al.) and the Guild for Psychological Studies in California, USA, whose seminars on the life and early records of Jesus opened my mind and led to a fascination with alternative ways of thinking about and reflecting on familiar biblical passages.

We are going to look at other ways of thinking about some well-known scripture passages based in part on how they might have been heard and received by the original listeners to the Aramaic language or in their culture of origin.

Jesus repeatedly challenged the common understandings of his day. 'You have heard that it was said… But I tell you…' (Matthew 5:21–43).

In the presence of holy mystery, reflect on your readiness or reluctance to explore understandings different from those you have been taught, and ask for open eyes and heart.

Good tree, bad tree

Bible study

Read Matthew 7:15–20.

> *Every good tree bears good fruit, but the bad tree bears bad fruit. A good tree cannot bear bad fruit, nor can a bad tree bear good fruit… you will know them by their fruits.*
> vv. 17–18, 20

The word here rendered as 'good' is, in Aramaic (the language Jesus would have spoken), *taba*. The roots of this word carry the sense of maintaining integrity and health – in tune, in time, in harmony, with everything – thus fit for purpose. The Aramaic word *bisha*, here translated as 'bad', implies that which is out of this harmony. It might mean something not yet ready for its purpose (immature or unripe) or that which has outlived its purpose – is over-ripe or rotten.

As an orchardist I learned that a young apple tree, in its first fruiting, bears just a few big, beautiful-looking apples which promise much but are dry and lacking in flavour. Only when it is mature is the tree able to produce mature, flavoursome fruit – in harmony with, and in fulfilment of, its purpose.

Thus a translation which more accurately reflects the original language might be something like: 'a mature tree bears mature fruit and an immature tree bears immature fruit'. Rather than being concerned with morals, this teaching is about times and seasons and appropriate expectations; about being fit for purpose and so in harmony with God's will.

Treat yourself to a piece of your favourite fruit, ideally fresh picked from the tree or the garden. Let it feed your senses of sight, touch and smell as you enjoy the anticipation of biting into it. As you take your first bite, do the taste and texture live up to your expectations?

What do the fruits of your life reveal about your ripeness or maturity in fulfilling God's purposes; your fitness or readiness to do so?

The paralytic and his friends

Imaginative

Carefully read Mark 2:1–12.

Try imagining the story as if you are the man on the mat. Where in you is the paralysed or palsied part (unable or unwilling to move, despairing, shaky, imprisoned, rejected or despised)? Who might be four companions you can, or need to, call upon to bring this part for healing? (These might be real people, heroic or biblical figures, qualities in yourself or lacking in yourself.) How might you call upon them for help? Imagine them struggling to place you in front of Jesus. How do you feel when they start digging through the roof? What does Jesus actually say to you? What do the scribes hear him say? (Does he claim to forgive sin himself?) How do you feel when he says, 'Stand up and take your mat and walk' or, perhaps more accurately, 'That which has carried [supported] you, you must now carry'?

What is it that you have depended on and must now carry? (Maybe an attitude of unforgiveness or resentment that you have justified by retelling and reliving the hurt you experienced.) How willing are you to do this? Find something (maybe a stone) to symbolise this, and carry it in your hand for a day. Notice how it hampers your ability to do other things. Ask God to help you let go of it.

A wedding at Cana

Reflective

Imagine yourself in someone's house, relaxing with a group of colleagues or friends. During a lull in the conversation, your host invites everyone to find a seat as you are about to hear a story. People settle down and an expectant hush falls on the room. The story teller begins, 'Once upon a time…' What is your immediate reaction to those words? What kind of story do you expect?

Just as the phrase 'Once upon a time' signals to many of us a particular kind of story, so does 'On the third day…' to a Judaic audience. It indicates a salvation story.

Remember the story of Abraham preparing to sacrifice Isaac (Genesis 22:1–19). Verse 4 begins, 'On the third day Abraham looked up…' At this point, the story is revealed as one of salvation. What difference does knowing this make to the way you hear the rest of the story?

John 2:1–11 begins, 'On the third day there was a wedding in Cana…' It is the only Gospel to include this story. What is going on here? Was the event unknown to the other Gospel writers or did they choose to omit it? If so, why?

If this is a salvation story, where do you see salvation in it? Why do you think the writer includes this story and why is it placed where it is within the Gospel? With what else does it resonate?

Recall some time in your life when what seemed to be a disastrous situation proved to be a time of salvation, growth or healing. Offer a prayer of thanksgiving for this experience.

Bethesda pool

Poetry

Some stories become so familiar that we always hear them in the same old way. We forget that, in the process of translation, we have lost any indication of the intonation, emphasis or emotion which might have been present. Read aloud the sentence, 'That man did not steal my purse' emphasising the word 'that'. Now repeat it with emphasis on 'man'. Continue reading with the emphasis on a different word each time. Note how the meaning changes.

Read John 5:1–14. Is this just about a physical healing or might there be a challenge to deeper wholeness hidden within it? (See also v. 14.)

He strolled in through the gate
and looked around;
noted each one of us,
and seemed to know each story.

He knew how long I'd been there,
how comfortable I'd become,
ambivalent – in my dependency –
about the possibility of change.

His eyes, searching my very depths,
discovered all I'd sought to hide
from myself, from others,
now from him.

Not one for wasting words,
he asked straight out:
'Friend, do you want
to be made well?'

I did not answer 'Yes.'
I sought, as usual, to escape
by blaming others
for my situation.

He would have none of it!
His voice stern and commanding
cut through my complacency,
His finger pointed at me.

'You,' he said, 'stand up.
Pick up your mat,
and walk!'
He pointed to the gate.

Imagine yourself as the man in this story. What might be the significance of Jesus' comment in verse 14 if addressed to you? Journal your response as a prayer.

Only through me

Bible study

I am the way, and the truth, and the life. No one comes to the Father except through me.
JOHN 14:6

Like many others, and for many years, I struggled with this text which seems to stand in stark contrast to the inclusive nature of Jesus' teaching and ministry whereby tax collectors and sinners, prostitutes and the unclean, even Gentiles are welcome in God's kingdom. Here he seems to endorse the exclusion of all but a select few.

Is this really Jesus' intention or has something been lost in translation? Is it possible that the way in which the text has been presented and used by the church to justify exclusivity has overlooked a deeper and a different message?

Much prayer and reflection over many years led me to wonder about a possible alternative meaning but, not being a biblical language scholar, I was unable to confirm its validity. The opportunity to do so arrived in the form of a young Anglican priest whose father is Maori and whose mother is Jewish. He had recently completed his doctoral thesis on biblical languages.

I asked him about this passage and whether the early texts would bear the translation, 'No one comes to the Father but by the work that I have accomplished' – namely, reconciling all things to God. (See 2 Corinthians 5:19, 'in Christ God was reconciling the world to himself', and John 19:30, the triumphant cry from the cross, 'It is finished.' That is – completed, accomplished.)

My young colleague's eyes lit up as he replied, 'Actually, that is a much more accurate translation.'

What is your heart response to this understanding?

Do you love me?

Imaginative

Read John 21:15–17.

Shakespeare, in Sonnet 43, wrote 'How do I love thee? Let me count the ways.' Unlike some other languages, English has only one word (love) to describe a variety of relationships and this has had a profound effect on our reading of this text. It appears that Jesus repeatedly asks the same question and doesn't listen to Peter's repeated reply – uncharacteristic though that may be – but, once again, something significant has been lost in translation.

The Greek language uses different words for different kinds of love – *agape* (unconditional love), *philia* (love of a friend), *philadelphia* (brotherly love), *philanthropia* (love of humanity) among others.

According to the Greek text Jesus asks Peter (v. 15), 'Simon, son of John, do you *agape* [unconditionally love] me more than these?' and Peter replies, 'Yes, Lord, you know that I *phileo* you [love you as a friend].'

In the next exchange, Jesus asks the same question and Peter gives the same reply. Then Jesus asks 'Simon, son of John, do you [really] *phileo* me [love me as a friend]?' And Peter, no doubt with relief that Jesus has met him at the point where he is able to respond wholeheartedly, replies, 'You know that I am your friend.'

This is not the boastful, overconfident Peter who believes in his own invincibility, who claimed that he was willing to lay down his life for Jesus (John 13:37), followed by that infamous three-fold denial of acquaintance to save his own skin. Now, even Jesus' repeated invitation to over-reach himself is resisted with unaccustomed self-awareness and humility.

Walk and talk with Jesus, sharing the things that are important in your life right now. At some point he asks you, 'Do you love me unconditionally?' How do you want to reply? How can you, with integrity and honesty, reply?

God is…

Prayer

God is spirit, and those who worship him must worship in spirit and truth.
JOHN 4:24

The Aramaic word *ruha* (Hebrew *ruach*) can be rendered in English as spirit, wind, air or breath. While European Christianity assumes only one of these is appropriate in any given context, to the Eastern mind all are present simultaneously and interchangeably.

Read Genesis 2:7: 'Then the Lord God formed man from the dust of the ground and breathed into his nostrils the breath of life; and the man became a living being.' Try replacing the word 'breath' with air, wind, spirit. Notice the shift in feeling and understanding with each change. The same can be done with other texts such as Genesis 1:2, John 20:22 and Acts 2:1–4.

What might it be like to understand God as air and to worship in breath and truth? In a quiet space, relax and become aware of your body. Feel the rhythm of your breath flowing in and out. After a while, silently repeat 'You in me' on each inward breath and as you breathe out, 'And I in you'. 'You in me – and I in you'; breathing in God as air, and breathing out your breath into God. Gradually let the words fall away until simply breathing carries your prayer. God is indeed closer than the air we breathe. Maybe it is not impossible to 'pray without ceasing' as Paul instructs (1 Thessalonians 5:17).

The dishonest manager

Intercession

Read Luke 16:1–9.

Christians have often struggled with this story as, from our cultural perspective, it seems that Jesus is endorsing dishonesty and exploitation – and how do we reconcile that with the rest of his teaching? The confusion (it seems to me) is based in the translation from one culture to another very different one. We have to let go of our own cultural spectacles and expectations, and adopt those of the culture and time into which the story was spoken – that of an Eastern country some 2,000 years ago where it was common for officials (think of the tax collectors) to add their own cut to any debt they were collecting. While this may have been a generally accepted practice, it was, of course, open to abuse.

It seems this manager may have become a bit too greedy in the amounts he added to the original debts, and, since he is accused of squandering his master's property, he might have been dipping his fingers into that as well. When caught out, he goes to those from whom he has demanded exorbitant amounts and reduces them to something closer to the original debt.

Thus, though still motivated by self-interest he might be, he begins moving towards restoration of justice – a move which benefits all concerned. The debtor is relieved of the burden of exploitation; the master receives his due amount; the manager, while losing the profit he had hoped for, gains friends and support for his anticipated time of need. A win for everyone!

Yes – Jesus makes the point that there is a need to take as much care about preparation and provision for our spiritual wellbeing as we do for our material comfort, but there is also a redemption message in this story. God can turn all to good.

Make a list of situations (international, national or local) where exploitation or abuse of power cause you concern. Is there anything you can do to help address these? If so, make a commitment to become actively involved. Prayerfully invite God to begin the process of transformation and redemption – even if you cannot see the way ahead. Dare you pray, 'O God, work your perfect will in this – whatever the cost may be'?

In Jesus' name

Going out

What does it mean to act in the name of another?

Ambassadors are authorised to act in the name of their country's government. So long as their actions are in accord with the will of those they represent, they will be supported by the power and authority of their government. If, however, they choose to 'do their own thing' and claim to be doing it in the name of their country, there will be no support forthcoming and they will soon be seen to be fraudulent.

Jesus taught his followers to pray and act in his name (John 14:13–14; 15:16; 16:23–24). Clearly this means more than simply adding the words 'in Jesus' name' to any petition.

The word translated here as 'name' is the Aramaic *shem*, which also carries the meanings of light, sound or atmosphere – all of these are present. Each is an expression of the cosmic energy, vibrating in every subatomic particle, which burst forth at the moment of creation and is expressed in everything that is – seen and unseen. It found expression in the person of Jesus – as it does in you. To pray or act in the name of Jesus means, therefore, to open oneself to the flow of that life-giving energy and to use it as Jesus would. Only when our prayer accords with what Jesus would pray can we, with integrity, claim to be acting in his name.

Visit some favourite spot where you feel in touch with creation and take time to explore it with all your senses. What can you see (for example, how many shades of green?), hear, smell, feel? Recognise that all of it is, like you, an expression of God's creative, life-giving energy. Take time to relax into this. Breathe slowly and sense being one with all that is, being one with Christ in all creation. Offer your prayer from this space.

Be perfect

Creative

Be perfect, therefore, as your heavenly Father is perfect.
MATTHEW 5:48

In Western Christianity, this verse has usually been understood as a call, or even a demand, to attain a state of flawless, sinless perfection. It has often contributed to a sense of inevitable failure, helplessness and even condemnation.

The word rendered here as 'perfect' is the Greek word *teleios*. One of the root meanings of this is a sense of 'moving towards fulfilment of purpose' or 'being in the process of becoming' – constantly moving towards or becoming something more than we are at present. It is a call to growth and change rather than to a static finite condition. It calls to mind Jeremiah's vision of the potter working clay – 'Just like the clay in the potter's hands, so are you in my hand' (Jeremiah 18:6).

I see the potter enjoying the feel of the soft clay, responsive and pliable; delighting in shaping and reshaping it; no final shape envisaged, no perfect product planned; the delight is in the moulding of the clay within the hand.

It seems, therefore, that the call to 'be perfect' is actually a call to growth and change from what we are to who and what we might yet become; a call to be open to whatever God may choose to do in and with us.

Take some modelling clay, plasticine, play dough or similar substance and work it in your hands until it becomes soft and malleable. Enjoy the freedom of shaping and reshaping it, playing without the need to make any particular product. Now, offer yourself as clay for God to play with and continually reshape.

Naming God

Creative

How can words describe that which is beyond all words? How can one define what is indefinable; name the un-nameable?

Language both reflects and shapes our thinking, so the words we use for God both reflect and shape the way we think about God.

How do you address God? What names do you use in prayer or in conversation? Make a list of all the names for God that you can think of and underline those which you actually use. What do you notice about this smaller group? How representative is it of the larger assortment?

The English word 'God' comes from an old word meaning 'good' – and this, over generations, has coloured our concept of God as removed from all evil. Much Eastern Christianity understands God as embracing evil, which is reflected in the name which Jesus would have used for God (apart from the intimate 'Abba'), which means variously 'the all', 'ultimate power/potential', 'sacred unity', 'the one with no opposite' or simply 'oneness'. It is the Aramaic word *Alaha*, clearly the source of the Arabic *Allah* but also of the Hebrew *Elohim*. The root of the word is *El* or *Al*, which is the definite article in Aramaic, Hebrew and Arabic, implying that every 'the', every unique thing, expresses something of God.

How does this challenge or reinforce your concept of God?

It has been said that the invitation of the Spirit is always to a larger space; the invitation to a smaller space usually comes from fear.

In the image of God

Sally Smith

Made in the image of God

Introduction

We are made in the image of God. Genesis chapter 1 tells us this:

> *So God created humankind in his image, in the image of God he created them; male and female he created them.*
> GENESIS 1:27

We are **made**. God made you; he didn't just think it would nice to have a person and there you were. He thought about you, planned you and then made you. He breathed life into you. Take a few moments to allow that to sink in – God… made… you.

We are made **in the image** of God. God didn't just think of an interesting design for you; he used the best template he had available: himself. God used himself as the mould when he made you. What does that tell you about the relationship between you and God, and about what he must think when he looks at you?

We are made in the image of **God**. This goes beyond our being made in the image of our parents; it is God we are considering here. You are made in the image of **God**.

As the creator, God takes a pride in his creation. He saw that is was good (or in the case of humankind on the sixth day, 'it was very good').

Quietly and slowly read Genesis 1:26–31. As you read, hear God saying the words to you personally, receive his blessing and hear him say that everything he has made is very good.

Who is God?

Creative

We learn right in the first chapter of the Bible that we are made in the image of God. If I am made in the image of God, it might be worth considering who this God is, in whose image I am made. It is a question that God's people in the Old Testament and the disciples in the New Testament are often asking. They receive various answers, but we don't have something definitive that answers all our questions about God, and that in itself tells us something about who God is.

Take a piece of paper and a favourite pen. In the middle of the paper write 'God is...'

Then, fill the rest of the paper with your thoughts on who God is. You might want to include some Bible verses; remember, this is just for you, so don't worry about references, or half-remembered verses. You are building up a picture of who God is for you at this point in time. You might find it easier to draw or collage.

You might want to group some of your words or images when they contain some common ideas or themes.

You may have some ideas you wouldn't want to share with anyone because they seem too offbeat – that's okay.

You might prefer to try and draw something that represents the character and God-ness of God. What colours and shapes do you use? What does each part represent?

You can add to your ideas over the coming days.

When you are ready, stop and look at your work. Sit before this God and talk to him about who he is. You may want to praise him, or bow down before him, or just sit with this greatest of friends or father.

Who am I?

Creative

We think we should know ourselves, but we don't always, though we may have a better idea than many other people who know us. Our parents may still have an image of the child we once were; our work colleagues may see a different person to the person our best friend knows. We may let some people see certain aspects of ourselves, but keep these hidden from others. We are complex beings, and, after a lifetime of being me, I can still be surprised.

Draw an outline of a person on as large a piece of paper as you can manage. Write and draw inside the person things that make you, you. You could ask others to add to this if you feel comfortable doing so. Stick on pictures from magazines or photos of significant places or incidents. Don't just include the things you can and can't do, but add something of who you are, the essence of you as a person.

Ask God to remind you of aspects of you that you may prefer to forget, or that are hidden for some reason.

As you work, do not be judgemental of what you are producing. I have a quote above my desk from Ann Lamott – 'God loves you as you are, and far too much to leave you as you are.' God loves you like this, but he also loves the person he is helping you to become.

When you are beginning to think you might have finished, if you have done the 'Who is God?' section, return to that work. You are made in the image of God. There will be some overlaps between the two – these are the places where you are becoming the person God intended you to be. There will be some places where there is a great gap – these are the areas still under construction. Again, don't be judgemental. This is how it is, and God still loves you. Spend some time taking this in.

Tell God about the ways in which you would like to be more like him and ask for his help in making you become the person he intended you to be in these ways.

You might find you return to these images as you explore what it means to be made in the image of God. Do add more, and cherish the images you have of both yourself and of God.

Before you leave these images for today, spend time before them with this verse from 1 Timothy 4:4:

For everything created by God is good, and nothing is to be rejected, provided it is received with thanksgiving; for it is sanctified by God's word and by prayer.

A creator God

Creative/reflective

We were made by God. That statement alone suggests that God is creative. But we also know that God made the world, each tiny flower and ant, the bumble bee and the elephant, along with the cactus and the whale. God came up with stars and the sun, with oceans and mountains. What an immense diversity there is in God's creation!

We are made in the image of the creator God. For some, this is easy to accept – creativity comes naturally and they recognise their God-given talents. For others, this is less of a natural step.

Consider your creativity. If this is not easy, try thinking differently: do you create order out of chaos, or a friendly atmosphere, or confidence in others, or do you have the gift of making the perfect cup of tea or making people laugh?

Though God made us innately good, we are also given the freedom to use our God-given abilities in whatever way we want. So we can use our creativity to enhance the world, or to destroy it.

Think back over the last 24 hours. What have you made in that time? Remember the small as well as the obvious.

Make something simple now (a sandwich, plant a seed, create order from chaos, origami, knitting, a bonfire, etc.) As you create, remember the creator God in whose image you are made. What does your creation say about you, and what do your hands learn about the one who made you? Are you open to allowing God to continue his work of creation in you, however painful that might be? As you create, allow the creator to create in you anew.

Walking in paradise

Imaginative

God created man and woman within the context of the garden of Eden. He gave them all the creatures and plants to tend and look after. He invited man to name the animals and birds. In Genesis 3:8, we find God walking in the garden. He saw man and woman as equal in that place and both were able to walk together with God in the same place where he walked. We were made to walk with God in his creation.

It was the serpent who got it wrong when he said that if they ate the apple they would be like God. Adam and Eve did not need to do anything to be like God; they already were like God. God had made them like him. This likeness does not end with the fall. In Genesis 9, Noah is reminded that humans were made in God's image and that any injury done to man is an injury done to God. James (3:9) still sees people as being in the likeness of God when he describes how the tongue can curse 'those who are made in the likeness of God'.

Being like God is not something we need to strive for; it is something that is pure gift from God. He wants us to be like him, to grow more like him. When he looks at us, he sees himself.

Imagine entering through the gate to a beautiful garden. It might be a favourite garden you know well, or it might be an imaginary garden. Follow the path and enjoy the plants and the insects.

Notice the scents and the sounds. Wander slowly around, pausing to look at anything that catches your eye.

You then notice a presence next to you, walking alongside you and also enjoying what they see. Allow yourself to walk in step with this companion and then begin to share your experiences of the garden.

After a while, you begin to suspect that this is the gardener you are walking with. Learn from him and the wisdom and enthusiasm he is offering. Notice also how much you share in your love of what you see and discover.

As you return to the gate, the gardener turns to you and, in that moment, you recognise that he is not just the gardener, he is the Gardener, and you have been walking with God in his garden. How do you feel? What do you say?

When you are ready, return through the gate and reflect on your experience.

Missing the target

Creative

The word 'sin' literally means to fall short of the target. It was used by archers to describe the arrow that didn't hit the target. This definition gives a different perspective to the idea we are used to of sin being 'getting it wrong'. To miss the target is to have tried and generally to have been in the right direction. It suggests that it is possible to hit the target and that we were close. It sits well with the British love of those who have a go, even if they don't succeed.

Draw a series of concentric circles, like a target used by archers.

Draw, or cut out and stick on, some arrows, naming them with aspects of who you are and noting how close to the target each one lands. Which are close to living in the likeness of God, and which fall short of being like God?

Ask God how accurate you have been in your placing of your arrows. Is this how he sees you?

Ask for his help in making some of them land nearer the mark.

Made in community

Imaginative

As you, Father, are in me and I am in you, may they also be in us, so that the world may believe that you have sent me.
JOHN 17:21

From the beginning, we relate to a God who is community. God made the animals, water, stars, etc. and at the end of each day he saw that it was good. But when it comes to creating humankind, God says, 'Let us make humankind in our image, according to our likeness' (Genesis 1:26). When Jesus came to live on earth and was separated from his Father, he was still one with the Father; they remained in community, together. It is the community of God who made us in their image. So, in this image we are invited to join with the community of God.

Find a copy of Rublev's icon of the Trinity (you may have already found one to use in 'A window into the Trinity' on p. 43). Though usually known as representing the Trinity, the icon was originally painted as the three angels who appeared to Abraham by the oaks of Mamre, but we will be using it as a representation of God as Trinity.

Spend some time looking at the image before you. How does it feel to be in the presence of God?

One of the figures begins to invite you to join them at the table. You are made in the image of God and are a part of this family. You have a familial likeness and you have the right to be there at the table with those in whose image you are made. Notice how that feels.

If you are able, imagine approaching the table and sitting with God.

You might talk, or listen, or just spend time silently together.

Notice how you react to the individuals around the table, and to the gathered community.

What do you want to say to the God community?

When you are ready, leave the table.

Spend time remembering the experience.

You might want to write an account in your journal. Don't analyse or criticise, just cherish that experience, and remember, you are invited to join the table at any time.

Made as community

Creative

If God is community, and we are made in his image, to what extent are we also each an individual community?

I am a different person in different situations and with different people. The person I am with my closest friends would not be an appropriate person for arriving at work. The work person would not be ideal for chatting with a local shopkeeper. Spend a moment thinking of the different people you might be during a day. Maybe re-run yesterday and see who you were and who each person was with.

Those are the people I show to the world, but there is also a community inside me. There is the adult who takes control, the often-frightened child, the rebel who just says no, the contemplative who wants to find a quiet corner.

Draw some stick people to represent the many 'people' who make up 'you'. You might want to name them. Befriend them, accept them as an important part of who you are. Some may need encouraging, some quietening down, but treat each one with respect.

Add three more stick people – God Father, God Son and God Spirit.

Allow them to interact with the other figures already on your page. Listen in on some of the conversations. Notice the quality of the relationships that already exist.

When you are ready, step back and notice any changes in how you view the figures you have drawn, that make up you. Thank God for the richness of 'you' and for his presence in the midst of the 'you community'.

Called to perfection

Creative

In Matthew 5:48, Jesus says, 'Be perfect therefore, as your heavenly Father is perfect.' Desmond Tutu (*Made for Goodness*, p. 55) says, 'You can be as I created you to be, the visible likeness of the invisible.' Becoming perfect is not about achieving perfection, but becoming the person God intended you to be.

We are called to be like our perfect God, but how can we as humans become perfect? God is not calling us to be perfect.

Spend some time in front of a mirror.

What do you see? Have a good look at your face. You are made in the likeness of God.

Sit before God as the child he has made you, accepting that he made you in his image.

I praise you, for I am fearfully and wonderfully made. Wonderful are your works; that I know very well.
PSALM 139:14

You are altogether beautiful, my love; there is no flaw in you.
SONG OF SOLOMON 4:7

For we are what he has made us, created in Christ Jesus for good works, which God prepared beforehand to be our way of life.
EPHESIANS 2:10

Do you imagine that I did not know who you were when I made you, when I knit you together in your mother's womb? Do you think I planted a fig tree and expected a rose to bloom? No, child, I sowed what I wanted to reap.

Desmond and Mpho Tutu, *Made for Goodness* (HarperOne, 2011), p. 36

All are made in God's image

Going out

So God created humankind in his image, in the image of God he created them; male and female he created them.
GENESIS 1:27

It is not just Christians, or God's chosen people, who are created in the image of God; everyone is created in the image of God. Desmond Tutu describes how this was a central belief of Trevor Huddleston:

He had a profound belief in the doctrine of creation. He truly believed that we are all equally created in the image of God. He lived as he believed. Conscience met action in a gesture of godly perfection. For him it was the most natural thing to do: doff his hat to another child of God.

Desmond and Mpho Tutu, *Made for Goodness*

He lived this way, even when he (a white man) was doffing his cap to Tutu's mother (a black woman living in 1940s apartheid South Africa).

What would it be like to live out that belief that God created everyone in his image, and that if we are all made in his image, we are all created equal and everyone in the world is your brother or sister?

Go for a walk where you will pass lots of people. As you walk, try to notice as many people as possible as individuals. Remember that they, like you, are made in the image of God.

Acknowledge God's love for them as you pass and recognise that it is the same love as he holds for you. If this causes you to want to smile, or speak to those you pass, then follow this calling; they, like you, are made in the image of God.

Image by association

Prayer/going out

Parents can often be concerned about who their children make friends with. Everyone wants their child's full potential to be brought out, and often this can be a direct consequence of who their friends are. We will probably all be able to name examples where a child's friend has brought the best out of them (and perhaps vice versa), as well as examples of children who have 'fallen in with a bad crowd'.

In the same way, there may be some people you spend time with and come away seeing the world differently, or changed in some way. Spend some time thinking about the people you meet regularly and how they influence the person you are. They might enable you to become more like God, or they might take you away from becoming God-like. Think back to the last time you met them and how it felt to be with them. Consider also how it felt after you had met them.

There may be some people you have known in the past who have influenced the person you now are. Often teenage friends have a significant influence on us, as can the adults who were around for us at that time.

If we can be so influenced by the people around us, becoming maybe more like them, or being led to find new aspects of ourselves when we are with them, how much more will being in God's presence influence the person we are and how like him we become?

Spend some time just being with God. If you have done the 'Made in community' section, you might like to return to the icon and sit again with God Father, Son and Spirit, allowing yourself to become more like them as you sit. Or you might prefer to go to their house, a local church that is left unlocked during the day, and spend time sitting with God, being and becoming. Or it might be that you become more like God when you have been out in his creation, so go for a walk and allow nature to draw you into being in the image of God. However you find God, spend some time with him asking that you may become more like him.

Being in the image of God

Reflective

We are made in the image of God. It is not something we can alter or remove. We are not perfect, as God is perfect, but we have the basics there. It is through Christ and the Holy Spirit that we become more like God.

As with any creator, God wants the best for his creation. He wants us to be improving and getting closer to the perfection he has for us. But he doesn't look at us and see the imperfections, how much further there is still to go. No, he looks at us and sees the children he loves, the parts that are reaching perfection, and he longs, for our sakes, for us to be nearer to his image of us. If we let him, he will do this work in us.

> *But to all who received him, who believed in his name, he gave*
> *power to become children of God, who were born, not of blood*
> *or of the will of the flesh or of the will of man, but of God.*
> JOHN 1:12–13

You might want to consider the impact knowing you are made in
the image of God has on how you view yourself, others and God.
Then think about the impact this might have on your relationship
with yourself, others and God.

End this theme by sitting with the one in whose image you are
made, enjoying being with a likeness of yourself.

Finding God where you are

Eirene Palmer

Life to the full

Introduction

Where do you find God? There will be as many answers to that question as there are people. Just as we are all unique, individual and special to God, we all have our different ways of relating to him. A good analogy would be to say that I love my husband absolutely, and I also love my children absolutely. My love for each is the same but different.

Jesus tells us in John 10:10 he came 'that they may have life, and have it to the full'.

A full life means being in touch with what brings you to life, opening you up and helping you to feel deeply connected with both yourself and with God. A full life feels real and authentic and comes from a place inside that longs and yearns for God and reaches out to him from the heart and feeling rather than head and thinking.

God is totally and completely interested in all of us – even and especially the parts that are hidden (maybe from ourselves) and he wants to help us to relate to him in these deep places. He is present in everything that we are and everything that we do, not just the few hours a week we spend at church or in our myriad other activities. Not that God isn't thrilled about our work for him, but he longs to be engaged in every aspect of our lives, and that means he can be found there too: in the places where we feel connected, where we feel most at ease and most truly ourselves.

For many years, I assumed that God was only to be found in one particular kind of prayer – the sort where you presented him with a list and hoped he would tick some of them off. But then God and I began to have a different kind of conversation. I began to realise that God was interested in the things I was interested in and that God was there for me in my love of music.

Another way of thinking about this could be to consider the things which close us down and the things which open us up. We all know the feeling we have when we are asked to do something we find wearisome or difficult and, even though we may be able to do it, it feels like hard work and is time-consuming. The things which open us up feel life-giving, they come easily and we want to do more and more of them. I am not a seamstress, and sewing a button on my husband's shirt makes me irritable and frustrated. But I am a musician, and picking up my recorder to play a sonata fills me with peace and joy. To me, that's a kind of prayer.

Take a moment to consider what brings you to life. Try not to think too much, just sit and relax and let the answer come to you. Where do you feel most relaxed and happy? Is it in walking in the hills or painting in oils? Listening to a piece of music? Singing in a choir? Building an extension? Playing with children? Swimming? Take the opportunity to consider this more deeply as you go about your daily activities and notice the things which make you feel more alive.

As you consider different ways of being in touch with what brings you to life, and so connect with God in the things you enjoy, notice your response to what is happening and to the God who journeys closely with you.

Find a symbol

Creative

To help focus on the idea of what brings you to life, look for a symbol which distillates this idea to you. It may be a particular verse or passage from the Bible. It may be a poem or a CD to represent a piece of music. It may be a photo, a recipe or any object – in fact, it can be anything at all! Finding a symbol that fits means that we capture the essence of 'where we're at'. This process can really help us to focus on what's happening for us in the present.

You may also like to write just a few words as explanation of what this means to you. This will help your reflections on this theme and enable you to see how, if at all, your perceptions have changed or developed by the end of this theme.

Place your symbol somewhere where you can easily dwell on it over the next few days. This may be in your prayer space, in the kitchen, next to your bed – anywhere it will catch your eye and lift your heart with its life-giving connection.

What brings me to life?

Reflective/creative

What brings YOU to life? What stirs in you that sense of happiness, joy, of being connected, of feeling totally yourself? These can be everyday activities that we take so much for granted, but which we don't sometimes realise how much they sustain us. It could be baking, music, art, cooking, swimming, writing, etc. Take some time to make a list of the things that bring you to life. Be open and honest with yourself as you work through this – it is your own private list unless you choose to share it with others. You don't have to create your list in words; you could use pictures, colour, or anything which brings you to life!

If you find joy in pictures and colour, draw yourself in a picture frame and surround it with illustrations of the things which awaken you.

If you knit, start a piece where each row and each colour represents something dear to you.

If you are a writer, write your list. Use words to express your creativity, to paint colours and textures, sounds and feelings. If you find you can't stop – don't!

Or just make a list!

As you work, notice how it feels to think about these things.

A way of prayer

Creative

Once you have your list of things that bring you to life, use it as a way of prayer. It doesn't matter how long or short your list is. Some may have a list of 20 things, others may have three or four. It's your list and it isn't up for discussion with anyone else. Pick one thing from your list, just one, and use it as a way of prayer today. Consciously invite God to be present with you in what brings you joy. Take God swimming with you, sing with him and hit the high notes, show him your favourite trees on your walk, let him join in the words of 'The Wheels on the Bus' with your two-year-old. God wants to be present in all of it. He wants to play with you!

Talk to him as you do your activity and allow him space to talk to you. Enjoy his presence with you.

Journalling

Spotlight

Journalling is popular these days and is an excellent way of recording our lives. It always has been, and we have some wonderful examples in the writings of Samuel Pepys, Anne Frank, Virginia Woolf and Alan Bennet to name but a few. But many of us scribble away in the privacy of our own rooms, recording our responses, our activities, our feelings, our accomplishments, our existences, our days. Philip Larkin reminds us that days are where we live, and keeping a journal is a way of catching them, keeping them, embracing them so we can look back and see where we have been and how far we have travelled.

Whether or not you already keep a journal, think afresh of how you might use it as a way of being with God. Many already use journalling as a way of prayer, but I invite you to think about either starting a journal with your list of what brings you to life – or including it in your journal if you already have one. Journalling isn't necessarily just writing. Be creative! Think outside the box. The important thing is to choose a way that brings you to life and that feels natural to you. That way it won't become a chore.

A journal takes on richness if you can add variety to it. Don't feel restricted to just writing a daily log. There are many other sources of material you can use. Include anything that speaks to you about your journey, either of your own making or materials from other sources, such as prose, poems, prayers, scriptures, letters, unsent letters, letters to God, articles from papers and magazines, quotes, stories, metaphors, course materials, passages from books, photocopies or whatever else appears relevant for you.

You don't have to restrict yourself to written materials. Use graphic material as well, such as sketches, doodles, painting, art, cartoons, photographs, icons, postcards, mind maps, diagrams, cut and paste, scrapbooking or whatever works for you. The important thing to remember is to express yourself openly.

You could also keep your journal electronically. This has some advantages. It is easy to add graphics, photos, links to websites and other media. You can also incorporate music and videos and it allows you to cut and paste materials from sites such as Pinterest and Facebook.

The parable of the sower

Meditative

Read Matthew 13:1–9.

This well-known Bible passage talks about the environment needed to help seeds grow. Rocky, shallow, thorn-infested places were all useless because the seeds could not put down roots and thrive. We too need to consider creating surroundings which enable us to flourish. Having identified those things which bring us to life, we need to nurture them and give them the best possible chance to fill our lives with healthy, nutritious God-given joy.

This isn't about having a big house, a banker's income or a wonderful extended family. It's about taking care of yourself as best you can, looking at how you live and making the most of your circumstances. Everyone can be kind to themselves and make small changes to nurture that flame or flicker inside of what brings them to life. Jesus himself carried no possessions and yet said, 'I have come that they may have life, and have it to the full' (John 10:10).

Think about how you can make the space in which you live into a life-giving space. Home for me is my safe space and it's important to me to make it a place where I can just be. It needs to be cosy and welcoming. I enjoy textures, colours, soft furnishings, pictures, candles, light and warmth. It's a lovely safe space to retreat to at the end of the day. I close the door, make a mug of tea and curl up on the sofa with a good book, wonderful music and chocolate. Your space may already feel like that for you, and if so, note and cherish those things about your space which do this.

Where is your safe space? Go into your space, whether it is home, a place of worship or somewhere else that helps you feel secure. How do you feel in that space? Breathe deeply and allow yourself to touch on those things which hold you and bring you to life. Let God speak to you. Know that God is there with you in your space. He wants you to be relaxed and restored by not doing much at all. Let him enfold you. Enjoy his presence as you reach out to him and he reaches back.

What brings me to life?

Reflective

In the 16th century, St Ignatius of Loyola, a young Spanish soldier and aristocrat, was compelled to follow Christ after nearly being killed on the battlefield. He wrote 'The Spiritual Exercises', the cornerstone of Ignatian spirituality which are a series of contemplative practices to help a retreatant understand their relationship to God and the world. The exercises use the 'Examen', which is a way of being in touch with what brings you to life, or deadens you. You are invited each day to ask yourself the question, 'For what am I most grateful today?' or, 'For what am I least grateful?' Or, to put it simply, 'When was I happy today?' and 'When was I sad?'

Being in touch with ourselves isn't something we are encouraged to consider in our busy 21st-century whirl of life. Life seems to be about doing rather than being. But using the Examen can help us to discover what we are really feeling – deep down in the places where we are most unaware of ourselves – and bring that to God very simply. Just ask the question:

'For what am I most grateful today?'

Sit for a while and reflect on your day. Even the most mundane day is unique because it will never happen again. What has been good about today? Just allow your day to wash over you and take a moment to notice and reflect on those things that were good and positive. However small it may feel at times, there will be something good about today. Sit with God and savour what brought you to life today.

Then say, 'Thank you, God.'

It can be a helpful practice to take time each evening to consider what you are most grateful for that day. You could record it in some way. You can write or draw it in your journal, or you can post it on Facebook or Twitter if you want to share it.

What deadens me?

Reflective

Considering what you are least grateful for today, what closes you down or what deadens you might seem like the negative, pessimistic bit, but in fact it is another way of being in touch with yourself and naming those things which sap your energy. Doing this can free this energy up for you to use in more productive ways, bringing to light those areas of your life which need reviewing or changing.

Sit quietly by yourself in your safe space. Allow yourself to breathe deeply and let God gently bring to you the things about today which have made you sad or closed you down in some way. Don't be judgemental about your responses – your response, whatever it is, is valid. God knows that there are moments in our life when we feel desolate, times for which we cannot feel grateful. Quietly name them, either out loud or in your mind to God and let him hold you as you acknowledge these feelings.

Sometimes we can't change our desolation, but by sitting with it at the end of the day and naming it to God, we take away just a little of its power to overwhelm us. If we can, we could name it to a good friend or family member, or a supportive group. If that isn't possible, telling God, either verbally, through playing music, or by writing or drawing in a journal can ease its ability to hurt.

It isn't always possible to only do the things which bring us to life – the car needs to be cleaned, housework and ironing done, bills paid, and there are people in our lives that we need to care for, even if they don't bring us to life at times. But, as far as possible, with consideration and compassion – try to identify the things which give you life – and do more of them while minimising the activities which drain you and close you down. Remember – God is especially in those areas of our life where we struggle for joy.

Using the Bible to bring us to life

Imaginative

When I was growing up, reading the Bible was a serious business. It was declaimed from the front of the church, usually in the Authorised Version, and seemed to be at times quite incomprehensible. It has taken time to change my attitudes and feelings about reading Bible passages.

St Ignatius developed a way of Bible reading which centres on contemplation of the Gospels. The reader is invited to use their imagination to reflect on a Gospel passage. All five senses are involved as they imagine the scene in their mind's eye and bring the scene to life.

Read the story of Zacchaeus in Luke 19:1–10.

Now try to imagine the scene. Use all of your senses to see, hear, touch, taste, smell. What can you see? Can you hear the noise of the crowd? Feel people jostling for position, pushing against you, trying to find the best vantage point to see Jesus?

Visualise yourself in the Gospel story. Don't seek intellectual insights – stay with the imagery. Use your senses to see, touch, feel and hear.

Notice if you are drawn to a particular part of the story.

You may find yourself becoming one character in the story. That's fine, go with where that leads you.

Notice how you feel at different points in the story.

When the story is finished, talk to God about your experience and listen to what God is saying to you.

Nourishing our roots – do more of it

Going out

Jesus wants us to be whole and happy, restored in both body and mind, able to face each day with energy and hope, not weighed down by impossible demands and duties.

Read Matthew 11:28–29.

A useful image for this is to imagine yourself as a tree. If your branches are going to be full and healthy and blossoming, able to sustain and hold all the different competing demands and components of your life, you need to have strong, firm and steady roots to support them.

Go outside and, if you are able, gently dig up a weed or an unwanted small plant by its roots and shake off the soil. Now you can see the part of the plant that is usually hidden from view. What do the roots look like? Notice how they are different from the part of the plant that grows above the surface. Look at the intricacies of the roots, absorbing nutrients from the soil in order to store them as food and then delivering them to the plant so that it can grow strong and healthy.

The roots of the plant you are holding anchor it into the ground. Where are your anchors? What helps you to grow? Sit a while with your plant and let God speak to you of what sustains and feeds you. Be gentle with yourself, just as you are gentle with your plant.

Nurturing yourself – spirit and body

Creative/going out

One way of nurturing yourself which can be hugely beneficial is to develop a practice of gratitude over a period of time. This is about consciously saying 'thank you' for the things which feed you and bring you to life. As you do this, contemplate the gifts which God has given you, and take time to savour them and enjoy their richness.

Here are two ways in which you can practise gratitude – try both or choose the one which best suits your interests and personality.

The gratitude garland

Take a long piece of ribbon or string – about three times the length that your finished garland will be as you are going to make knots in it. You might want to choose something to tie to the end to 'anchor' it like a pom-pom, bell, or large bead.

Choose something on which you can write, or draw or stick pictures on (or all three), such as a parcel label. You may want to cut it into a shape – a heart or a bird maybe. Make a hole with a hole punch, and thread ribbon or string through that so you can attach it to the garland.

Then be creative! Think about those things for which you are grateful in your life. This could be people or events or what has happened in the past year, or month, or week or today. Write or draw on your label to illustrate this and then attach it to the garland. You may want to attach beads or sequins or leaves between the labels to separate them.

When the garland is finished, hang it up somewhere where you can see it each day – maybe in your prayer space – and say 'thank you'.

The gratitude walk

Or you could try a gratitude walk. Walking, as we know, is extremely beneficial for health and you may already be walking half an hour or so each day. Try taking the first five or ten minutes to be mindfully grateful. Look around you. Notice the trees, the birds, the children playing, the friendly dog. Notice them rather than just seeing them.

When you get back, make notes in a notebook of something that has particularly struck you, such as the pink blossom on that tree, the greenness of the leaves, the smell of wet grass. Or take photos as you go of things you are grateful to God for. Do this daily and make the practice of gratitude part of your life.

'Just as I am'

Reflective

In this section we have been considering what brings us to life, what closes us down and reflecting on the God who wants only good things for his children. He wants us to be happy and talk to him in ways which fill us with joy and enable us to grow.

Spend some time reflecting on your prayers and meditations through this theme. Look back over your discoveries. Did you find a new or different way of talking to God? Did he make himself known, not only in a way of prayer that is familiar, but in the unfamiliar too? What did God enjoy doing with you?

If you kept a journal, look back over your entries. You may like to write your key ideas on Post-it notes and put them up in places where you will see them every day. Remind yourself gently that God is interested and involved in everything you do, all the time, and doesn't want to be confined to church or to the boundaries of a prayer time (though he does enjoy these spaces with you as well).

Look at the symbol of what brings you to life you chose in the 'Find a symbol' section (p. 109). How has this accompanied you through these reflections? You may like to choose something else to be with you as you journey on.

God loves the whole of you and wants to join you in everything that brings you to life. As St Teresa of Avila said in the 16th century, 'A soul which gives itself to prayer, either much or little, should on no account be kept within narrow bounds.'

God can't be limited to 'narrow bounds'. He is right where you are and waiting to be found.

Journal page

As a Child

Phil Steer

Praise

> *From the lips of children and infants you have ordained praise.*
> MATTHEW 21:16, NIV

I belong to a church in which the children are encouraged to come to the front to sing and dance, and wave flags and streamers during the times of praise and worship. Now doubtless it is a good thing that they are able to take part in the services in this way, rather than having to sit quietly bored while we adults sing in our serried ranks. It is good that they can feel welcome in church, able to be themselves rather than having to be on their best behaviour. But one has to ask: is what they're doing really praise? Do the children truly understand what they are singing or appreciate the one to whom their 'praise' is directed? Isn't it just that they enjoy this time for its own sake? Would it make any difference if they were singing and dancing to regular pop songs? Quite frankly, is it really any different to being at a party or disco (if not quite so much fun)?

A very similar question might be asked of the children whom we find with Jesus in the temple courts after his triumphal entry into Jerusalem, shouting 'Hosanna to the Son of David!' (Matthew 21:15). Did they really know what they were saying? Did they have any idea of who Jesus was, or what he had come to fulfil? Or were they simply joining in the fun, caught up in the excitement of the moment, parroting the praise of the crowd that had welcomed Jesus as he came riding on a donkey (Matthew 21:8–9)?

Certainly the chief priests and teachers of the law thought so: 'Do you hear what these children are saying?' they asked him (Matthew 21:16). Of course, they didn't even accept the truth of the acclamation – that Jesus was the son of David, the Messiah who was to come – but it was undoubtedly doubly disturbing for them to hear his praises sung by naïve, impressionable children.

Jesus' reply is telling: 'Have you never read, "From the lips of children and infants you have ordained praise"?' He is completely unconcerned by the fact that the children might not understand just who he is, might not understand the meaning of what they are shouting. This matters not at all; Jesus welcomes their praise. Indeed, more than simply welcomes, for he declares that God has specifically chosen children and infants to praise him. The praise of children is indeed true praise.

The purpose of praise is to glorify God; the focus of our praise is Jesus himself. This might seem an unnecessarily obvious thing to say, and yet it is very easy to slip into seeing praise from our point of view rather than God's, to allow the focus to drift away from God and on to ourselves. And this can happen from the seemingly best of intentions. We want to be sure that our praise and worship is more than just words – we want it to be meaningful and heartfelt; we want to 'engage with God' and 'touch his heart'. But the unintended consequence can be that we judge the success of our praise by how we ourselves feel. Did we feel in a 'good place' with God? Did we sense something of his presence? Did our praise 'rise to the heavens' or did it seem to bounce back to us off the ceiling?

But ultimately none of this much matters, because praise is not about us; it is about God. The purpose of praise is to glorify God – and if he is glorified then the praise is acceptable to him. Children may understand little of what they are saying or of the one to whom they direct their praise, but in their 'ignorance' and innocence they give Jesus the honour that is due his name. God's praise is being sung, and so he is being praised. This is in stark contrast to the religious leaders of Jesus' day, who for all their learning were unwilling to do the same (and indeed, it could be argued that their learning was actually an obstacle to them recognising Jesus for who he is).

If we still think that our understanding and awareness of God is an important factor in the reality of our praise, then we need only consider the fact that God does not need us to praise him. He could call forth praise from the very fabric of our buildings: from the bricks and stones, the roof and floor, the windows and doors. For as Jesus replied to the Pharisees when they told him to rebuke his disciples for praising God: 'If they keep quiet, the stones will cry out' (Luke 19:40).

Praise could continue on quite happily without us, just as it has done from the very dawn of creation. As the psalmist writes, 'The heavens declare the glory of God; the skies proclaim the work of his hands. Day after day they pour forth speech; night after night they display knowledge' (Psalm 19:1–2).

We tend to take this to mean that the peoples of the world can learn of God and his glory through the splendours of the natural world; and of course this is right. But, first and foremost, the heavens declare the glory of God not to us, but to the one who created all things. His praise has been ringing out across the vast expanse of the universe ever since he spoke it into being.

In another psalm, the call to praise is directed specifically at creation itself: angels and heavenly hosts; sun, moon and stars; sea creatures and ocean depths; lightning and hail; snow, clouds and winds; mountains and hills; fruit trees and cedars; wild animals and cattle; small creatures and flying birds; kings, princes and rulers; young men and maidens; old men and children. 'Let them praise the name of the Lord, for his name alone is exalted, his splendour is above the earth and the heavens' (Psalm 148:13).

Animals and inanimate objects offering praise to God? How can this be? They certainly do not understand what it is they are doing;

they cannot consciously and deliberately offer praise. And yet, by simply being the things that God created them to be, and doing the things God created them to do, praise flows naturally from them. If creation can naturally and unconsciously praise God, then so can little children and so can we.

Now, please understand, I am in no way advocating the mindless singing of theologically suspect songs. When the children in the temple courts shouted 'Hosanna to the Son of David', they might not have understood the truth of what they were saying, but it was the truth nonetheless. We praise God for who he is, not for who he is not.

Jesus told the Samaritan woman, 'The true worshippers will worship the Father in spirit and truth, for they are the kind of worshippers the Father seeks' (John 4:23). But the word 'truth' means so much more than doctrinally correct. Jesus came 'full of grace and truth' (John 1:14) to be 'the way and the truth and the life' (John 14:6). Everything that he said, everything that he did, everything that he was demonstrated the way that things are meant to be; this is the meaning of 'truth' in its fullest sense. And so, if we are to praise God 'in spirit and in truth', then we must do so with the right attitude and without pretence; for God does not look at the outward appearance, he looks at the heart (1 Samuel 16:7). Indeed, it is not bad doctrine in song that causes God to reject our praise, but rather a lack of 'truth' in our lives.

The words of the prophet Amos should serve as a warning to us whenever we are tempted to become too self-satisfied and self-absorbed with our praise: 'I hate, I despise your religious feasts; I cannot stand your assemblies... Away with the noise of your songs! I will not listen to the music of your harps. But let justice roll on like a river, righteousness like a never-failing stream!' (Amos 5:21, 23–24).

Praise and worship that is not offered 'in spirit and in truth' will not be acceptable to God, regardless of how theologically sound it might be, while, conversely, the occasional doctrinal digression is unlikely to be cause for too much concern. The great I AM does not need us to remind him who he is; he knows that full well.

Indeed, it is perhaps we ourselves who suffer most from singing songs containing poor theology. These can reinforce in us misapprehensions of just who God is and what he does, and this in turn can affect how we relate to God and how we seek to live our lives in him. This being the case, I can imagine Jesus graciously accepting such praise, while at the same time drawing alongside us and gently seeking to lead us into more of his truth.

In his essay 'First and Second Things', the writer C.S. Lewis considers the importance of priorities, of ensuring that we put first things first. We cannot obtain 'second things', Lewis says, by seeking them for their own sakes, by making these the objects of our desire. Rather, we must value and pursue the 'first things' – the greater things – and then these 'second things' will follow.

This principle holds true in many different areas of our life and faith, and it certainly holds true with our praise. If we seek after 'reality', then we risk missing both the reality we seek and, more importantly, the true praise that God desires. But if we seek simply to offer our praise to God, then he will truly be praised, and through such praise he may graciously grant us a glimpse of the reality that we desire.

The praise of little children reminds us that true praise is all about God. It also reminds us that it comes from those who are truest to themselves, who are closest to being the people that God created them to be. So let us become like little children, and learn from them, and join with them in the joy of instinctive, spontaneous, unselfconscious praise.

The Corrymeela Community

Pádraig Ó Tuama
Leader of the Corrymeela Community

How can prayer and violence be in the same sentence?

How can prayer and violence be in the same life?

How can prayer and violence be in the same place?

These are questions that have followed the Corrymeela Community since our founding in 1965.

Corrymeela was founded by the Revd Ray Davey. He had been a prisoner of war in Dresden and his release came with the destruction of that city in February 1945. Freedom came in the ruins of a city, and Ray returned to Belfast, a city fresh into a new jurisdiction, and saw that the city was aching towards its own ruin.

The border in Ireland was created in 1921, where British presence withdrew from 26 of the 32 counties of Ireland, but remained in six of the nine counties of Ulster, the northernmost province of Ireland. There are shelves in libraries weighed down with explanations, justifications, reasons, defences and critiques of this choice. Some saw it as a temporary solution; others saw it as a permanent solution. What was previously called 'The United Kingdom of Great Britain and Ireland' was renamed 'The United Kingdom of Great Britain and Northern Ireland'. Some saw this as an acceptable compromise; others didn't. An uneasy century of British–Irish relations was launched.

And so, Ray returned from Dresden to a city in a jurisdiction that was not yet 25 years old in its delineation. Relations within the new border were not easy, nor were they easy between Britain and Ireland. Ray had seen humanity's capacity for inhumanity in the horrors of war and was determined that his beloved Belfast would not need to see annihilation in order to achieve resolution.

So great a hope, and it is impossible to imagine what would have happened in Northern Ireland without great people of peace, like Ray and so many others.

Ray worked as a chaplain in Queen's University in Belfast, and all the while was taking inspiration from new emerging European communities of faith and peace for appropriate forms in the north of Ireland. He, with students, visited many, and had many small starts at community living: friendships of lifetimes were formed. In 1965, when he heard of a piece of land for sale on the very north coast of Ireland, near Ballycastle, on six acres of land for which the traditional name was *Corrymeelagh*, he went into full gear. He was 50 by then. He had many contacts and hundreds of people had been through his chaplaincy programmes. He fundraised the money in less than a month, bought the property with its ramshackle building and the Corrymeela Community was born: a place for people to come together to pray, to work, to speak of their divisions, to vote differently but to hope in a way that benefited the mutual flourishing of each other.

So much story! But for Corrymeela, story is one of our beginnings. Every person who has been a victim or perpetrator of division has a story. Those stories are sometimes heartbreaking to hear; sometimes those stories are a relief to hear; sometimes those stories hurt to hear; sometimes those stories change us. So story – story sharing, storytelling and story listening – is a spiritual practice. Another spiritual practice is hospitality. At Corrymeela, we form temporary communities of dialogue, argument, faith and food. We pass the salt to people we disagree with. We wash dishes alongside someone whom we never thought we'd stand – never mind work – alongside.

Corrymeela works with 10,000 people a year on programmes of peace and reconciliation. We welcome people from all walks of life, all viewpoints on faith and humanity. As a Christian community, we see that the table is always made better by people who see things in ways different to us and, indeed, the 'us' in this sentence is a false construct. The Corrymeela Community is made up of individuals and we revel in our own disagreements. The word 'Corrymeela' was originally explained to Ray as meaning 'hill of harmony'. This delighted the young community. However, ten years later in 1975, an etymologist of Old Irish explained to the community that it meant something more like 'lumpy crossing place'. By this stage, the Troubles had broken out, and hundreds had been displaced, killed, wounded and bereaved. Communities had fractured and Corrymeela had lost members, friends and family. Hill of Harmony was a grand vision. Lumpy crossing place was a fine start. In this way, we see ourselves as very much a community following the Celtic understanding of Christianity: the land itself is part of our healing and our hope. The name of the place where we meet is a name that might help us.

Corrymeela members are people of all ages and Christian traditions who, individually and together, are committed to the healing of social, religious and political divisions that exist in Northern Ireland and throughout the world. Our community is a dispersed community of individuals from many walks of life and many approaches to faith and values who, in their daily lives, commit to the values and vocation of being a member of the Corrymeela Community – by this we mean incorporating commitment, practice and values into everyday life.

Our daily prayer is short and simple. We have 31 texts from the Gospels – texts that trace the theme of *do not fear* through the birth, life, relationships, torture, murder, burial and resurrection of Jesus. We reflect on this text for a short moment, and reflect on our world today. Then we pray a short prayer for courage.

Courage is a word firmly rooted in the human body. Coming from the Latin *cor*, meaning 'heart', we realise that fortitude is usually felt in the body, and that courageous individuals can help the hearts of others by their courage. Courageous communities are sustained by the courage of some that help the courage and generosity of all. Our own prayer chapel at Corrymeela is named after the heart too. We use the Irish word *Croí* (pronounced 'kree').

Corrymeela is people.

We are young people, middle-aged and old people.

We are people of doctrine and people of doubt.

We engage with the differences of our world.

We disagree with each other, and we seek to disagree agreeably.

We know we're part of the problems of the world.

We work hard to be part of the solution.

We are people of prayers and protest,

curiosity and questioning,

work and learning.

We are Corrymeela.

And you are always welcome.

Courage comes from the heart
and we are always welcomed by God,
the Croí of all being.

We bear witness to our faith,
knowing that we are called to live lives
of courage, love and reconciliation
in the ordinary and extraordinary moments
of each day.

We bear witness, too, to our failures
and our complicity in the fractures of our world.

May we be courageous today.
May we learn today.
May we love today.
Amen

If you would like to know more about the Corrymeela Community, visit the websites below:

www.corrymeela.org
www.twitter.com/corrymeela
www.facebook.com/corrymeela

BRF Quiet Days

BRF Quiet Days are an ideal way of redressing the balance in our busy lives. Held in peaceful locations around the country, each one is led by an experienced speaker and gives the opportunity to reflect, be silent and pray, and, through it all, to draw closer to God.

Here is the programme for 2018:

Thursday 10 May: 'From here to eternity' led by Bridget and Adrian Plass at Scargill House, Kettlewell, North Yorkshire BD23 5HU

Wednesday 6 June: 'Finding space to listen to God' led by Jennifer Rees Larcombe at House of Retreat, The Street, Pleshey, Chelmsford CM3 1HA

Wednesday 20 June: 'Finding ourselves in God: spiritual practices to root ourselves in Christ' led by Amy Boucher Pye at St Paul's Church, 50 Long Lane, Finchley, London N3 2PU

Tuesday 3 July: A teaching day on the theme of 'Pilgrims making progress: a day with Psalm 84' led by Tony Horsfall at The Mirfield Centre, Stocks Bank Road, Mirfield, West Yorkshire WF14 0BW

Wednesday 26 September: 'Give us this day our daily bread…' led by Debbie Thrower at Old Alresford Place, Alresford, Hampshire SO24 9DH

Monday 8 October: 'Be still and know… God's love' led by Claire Musters at Holy Trinity Centre, Maldon Road, Wallington S6 8BL.

For further details and to book, please go to **brfonline.org.uk/ events-and-quiet-days** or contact us at BRF, 15 The Chambers, Vineyard, Abingdon OX14 3FE; tel: +44 (0)1865 319700.

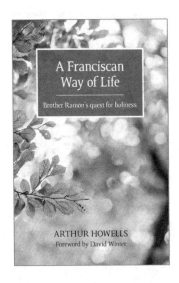

Brother Ramon, who died in 2000, was a man who delighted in life and people, and who chose solitude to practise the presence of God. This first biography, written by his friend, has warmth and spiritual insight. It tells of his life's pilgrimage, his quest for holiness as a Franciscan friar, his love of God and his influence on others. The selection from his writings which concludes the book illustrates his spiritual journey.

A Franciscan Way of Life
Brother Ramon's quest for holiness
Arthur Howells
978 0 85746 662 4 £8.99
brfonline.org.uk

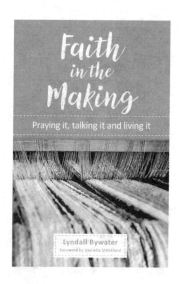

What does faith look like in practice today? In a world that is largely unsure and uncertain, how do we gain our confidence? *Faith in the Making* seeks the answer in the list of faithful heroes found in Hebrews 11. This accessible, devotional resource will inspire individuals and groups to live more confidently for God in today's world. Heroic faith is far more attainable than we often think!

Faith in the Making
Praying it, talking it and living it
Lyndall Bywater
978 0 85746 555 9   £7.99
brfonline.org.uk

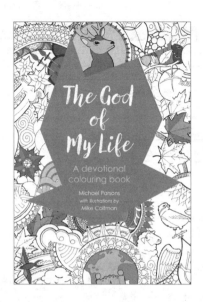

Doodling and colouring help many of us to be present in the moment, giving us more focus and aiding concentration. This unique book offers the chance to colour while reflecting on a psalm and so to concentrate unhurriedly on our relationship with the Lord. Many will find this book a helpful resource for a special kind of devotional time.

The God of My Life
A devotional colouring book
Michael Parsons
978 0 85746 584 9 £8.99
brfonline.org.uk

To order

Online: **brfonline.org.uk**
Tel.: +44 (0)1865 319700
Mon–Fri 9.15–17.30

Delivery times within the UK are normally
15 working days. Prices are correct at the time of
going to press but may change without prior notice.

Title	Price	Qty	Total
A Franciscan Way of Life	£8.99		
Faith in the Making	£7.99		
The God of My Life	£8.99		

POSTAGE AND PACKING CHARGES			
Order value	UK	Europe	Rest of world
Under £7.00	£2.00	£5.00	£7.00
£7.00–£29.99	£3.00	£9.00	£15.00
£30.00 and over	FREE	£9.00 + 15% of order value	£15.00 + 20% of order value

Total value of books	
Postage and packing	
Total for this order	

Please complete in BLOCK CAPITALS

Title .... First name/initials .... Surname ....

Address ....

.... Postcode ....

Acc. No. .... Telephone ....

Email ....

Please keep me informed about BRF's books and resources ☐ by email ☐ by post
Please keep me informed about the wider work of BRF ☐ by email ☐ by post

Method of payment

☐ Cheque (made payable to BRF) ☐ MasterCard / Visa

Card no. ☐☐☐☐ ☐☐☐☐ ☐☐☐☐ ☐☐☐☐ ☐☐☐☐ ☐☐☐☐

Valid from [M M] [Y Y] Expires [M M] [Y Y] Security code* ☐☐☐
Last 3 digits on the reverse of the card

Signature* .... Date .... / .... / ....
*ESSENTIAL IN ORDER TO PROCESS YOUR ORDER

Please return this form with the appropriate payment to:
BRF, 15 The Chambers, Vineyard, Abingdon OX14 3FE | enquiries@brf.org.uk
To read our terms and find out about cancelling your order, please visit **brfonline.org.uk/terms**.

QS0218

QUIET SPACES SUBSCRIPTION FORM

> All our Bible reading notes can be ordered online by visiting
> **biblereadingnotes.org.uk/subscriptions**

If you and a minimum of **four** friends subscribe to *Quiet Spaces* or BRF's other Bible reading notes (*New Daylight*, *Day by Day with God*, *Guidelines*, *The Upper Room*), you can form a group. What's so good about being in a group? You pay the price of the notes only – postage is free for delivery to a UK address. (All notes are sent to one address.) All group orders are invoiced. No advance payment is required. For more information, visit biblereadingnotes.org.uk/group-subscriptions or contact the BRF office.

Title _____ First name/initials _____ Surname _____

Address _____

_____ Postcode _____

Telephone _____ Email _____

INDIVIDUAL SUBSCRIPTION Please send *Quiet Spaces* beginning with the September 2018 / January 2019 / May 2019 issue (*delete as appropriate*):

	Quantity	UK	Europe	Rest of world
(per 3 issues)	☐	☐ £16.95	☐ £25.20	☐ £29.10

Total enclosed £ _____ (cheques should be made payable to 'BRF')

Please charge my MasterCard / Visa ☐ Debit card ☐ with £ _____

Card no. ☐☐☐☐ ☐☐☐☐ ☐☐☐☐ ☐☐☐☐

Valid from ☐☐☐☐ Expires ☐☐☐☐ Security code* ☐☐☐

Last 3 digits on the reverse of the card

Signature* _____ Date _____/_____/_____

*ESSENTIAL IN ORDER TO PROCESS YOUR ORDER

To set up a Direct Debit, please also complete the Direct Debit instruction on the reverse of this form.

GROUP SUBSCRIPTION (UK only) Please send *Quiet Spaces* beginning with the September 2018 / January 2019 / May 2019 issue (*delete as appropriate*):

Quantity ☐ (Current price per issue: £4.50)

Please invoice me: per issue / annually (*delete as appropriate*).

Please return this form to:
BRF, 15 The Chambers, Vineyard, Abingdon OX14 3FE

To read our terms and find out about cancelling your order, please visit **brfonline.org.uk/terms**.

The Bible Reading Fellowship is a Registered Charity (233280)

The Bible Reading Fellowship

Instruction to your bank or building society to pay by Direct Debit

Please fill in the whole form using a ballpoint pen and return it to:
BRF, 15 The Chambers, Vineyard, Abingdon OX14 3FE

Service User Number: | 5 | 5 | 8 | 2 | 2 | 9 |

Name and full postal address of your bank or building society

To: The Manager	Bank/Building Society
Address	
	Postcode

Name(s) of account holder(s)

Branch sort code

| | | – | | | – | | |

Bank/Building Society account number

| | | | | | | | | |

Reference number

| | | | | | | | |

Instruction to your Bank/Building Society
Please pay The Bible Reading Fellowship Direct Debits from the account detailed in this instruction, subject to the safeguards assured by the Direct Debit Guarantee. I understand that this instruction may remain with The Bible Reading Fellowship and, if so, details will be passed electronically to my bank/building society.

Signature(s)

Banks and Building Societies may not accept Direct Debit instructions for some types of account.

DIRECT DEBIT PAYMENT

You can pay for your annual subscription to our Bible reading notes using Direct Debit. You need only give your bank details once, and the payment is made automatically every year until you cancel it. If you would like to pay by Direct Debit, please use the form opposite, entering your BRF account number under 'Reference number'.

You are fully covered by the Direct Debit Guarantee:

The Direct Debit Guarantee

- This Guarantee is offered by all banks and building societies that accept instructions to pay Direct Debits.

- If there are any changes to the amount, date or frequency of your Direct Debit, The Bible Reading Fellowship will notify you 10 working days in advance of your account being debited or as otherwise agreed. If you request The Bible Reading Fellowship to collect a payment, confirmation of the amount and date will be given to you at the time of the request.

- If an error is made in the payment of your Direct Debit, by The Bible Reading Fellowship or your bank or building society, you are entitled to a full and immediate refund of the amount paid from your bank or building society.

- If you receive a refund you are not entitled to, you must pay it back when The Bible Reading Fellowship asks you to.

- You can cancel a Direct Debit at any time by simply contacting your bank or building society. Written confirmation may be required. Please also notify us.

How to encourage Bible reading in your church

BRF has been helping individuals connect with the Bible for over 90 years. We want to support churches as they seek to encourage church members into regular Bible reading.

Order a Bible reading resources pack
This pack is designed to give your church the tools to publicise our Bible reading notes. It includes:

- Sample Bible reading notes for your congregation to try.
- Publicity resources, including a poster.
- A church magazine feature about Bible reading notes.

The pack is free, but we welcome a £5 donation to cover the cost of postage. If you require a pack to be sent outside the UK or require a specific number of sample Bible reading notes, please contact us for postage costs. More information about what the current pack contains is available on our website.

How to order and find out more
- Visit **biblereadingnotes.org.uk/for-churches**.
- Telephone BRF on +44 (0)1865 319700 Mon–Fri 9.15–17.30.
- Write to us at BRF, 15 The Chambers, Vineyard, Abingdon OX14 3FE.

Keep informed about our latest initiatives
We are continuing to develop resources to help churches encourage people into regular Bible reading, wherever they are on their journey. Join our email list at **biblereadingnotes.org.uk/helping-churches** to stay informed about the latest initiatives that your church could benefit from.

Introduce a friend to our notes
We can send information about our notes and current prices for you to pass on. Please contact us.